EXTRAVAGANT ADVENTURES

SUE SINCLAIR

CONTENTS

ACKNOWLEDGMENTS

I would like to give God all the glory, right from the start as you read this book. I want to thank Him for the favour He has given to me, for the doors He has opened and for the incredible adventures He has allowed me to go on with Him.

I want to thank my family who have released, supported, encouraged and enabled me to go where God has called me to go. I know that you will reap a mighty blessing for all that you have given that nobody else knows about.

I want to thank all my fellow adventurers who have trusted God in me, travelled with me and made personal sacrifices to help us to journey together. Big thanks to all who are or who have been a part of the CWM Team since we began.

A huge thank you to all who have helped with the editing and publishing. Thank you Norma Dean, Ann Weaver, Pam Shaw, Liz Geddes, Jane Holloway, Michael Marcel, Denise Ashworth and especially David Powell my publisher. You will forever be my heroes!

ENDORSEMENTS

I have known Sue Sinclair for many years, and have been with her on some of her remarkable adventures. She is an ordinary woman, trusting and following an extra-ordinary God. Walking with Him into the hard, difficult situations - and seeing Him answer prayer - is part of the normal Christian life. Sue's testimony amply demonstrates that when one does, God fulfils His promises. Reading this book is like reading a modern-day "Acts of the Apostles". All glory goes to God - He really does "immeasurably more than all we ask or imagine", and uses ordinary people to do exploits, in unusual places and in unprecedented ways."

Brian Mills
Founder of Interprayer International Partnership, Author and International Speaker.

Extravagant Adventures is a book that will inspire, motivate and challenge. The stories it contains took place because Sue and her CWM friends decided to take God seriously, sought his face in the place of prayer and obeyed all that the Holy Spirit asked them to be and to do. It sounds simple and it is simple. Let us use this book as a springboard for our own adventures and

take Sue's encouragement to us all to 'choose life with Jesus, take a hold of the keys God has for you and choose to be an adventurer'.
Jane Holloway
National Prayer Director, World Prayer Centre.

Extravagant Adventures is a clear, compelling, clarion-call to follow the God who calls us not to waste our one and only life in trivial pursuits, but rather to give our life to Him and experience adventures beyond our imagining. Is this possible...? This book says it is. So why would you not...?"
Rev. John Kearns,
Old Roan Baptist Church, Liverpool

I do not mean it to be too grandiose when I suggest that here is a woman who is a latter day Joshua, standing at the Jordan river, knowing the cost of going forward, and recognising that the past has brought her to this place for this time. For Joshua stepping up to the place of leadership brought a realisation that he heard the word of the Lord. He had been honed and shaped through all his past experiences and came to this place knowing he was known. Hearing the word of the Lord and acting upon the word of the Lord are two different things. There are a surprising number of people who will tell you they hear the word of God come to them in different situations, but there are a surprisingly fewer number who actually go and do what has been said to them. Joshua, honed, readied and open to the things the Spirit of God brought from the highest heavens, now has to do it.

"Extravagant Adventures" shares the story of Sue going across her Jordan, and doing just exactly what she heard God say to do. It has taken her and her team to some remarkable places and had them do what seemed to be strange things. They were in fact just doing what they heard God say. Enjoy this "Extravagant Adventures" and then be bold and courageous as you go and join in with God in what you hear Him tell you to do!
Rev. Charles J. Finnie
Burnfoot, Hawick

FOREWORD

BISHOP ARNOLD MUWONGE

Here is my advice. Do not read this book!

That is unless you want your life to be changed!
Unless you want to read each page with a heart full of how great God is!
Unless you want to be inspired to live out your destiny...your own adventure with God
Unless you want to be encouraged that the God of heaven can transform your life, your community, your nation, if you place it in His hands.

Because Sue Sinclair is an inspiration and torch bearer! A fire carrier! A mighty warrior who walks humbly with her God!

She is a living testimony that where God finds willing hearts and an open space, He will do incredible things. And here, she shares the stories of walking her adventure with God.

I have had the privilege of ministering alongside Sue and the CWM team in Europe and Africa. I have seen their faithful obedience and passionate praying hearts. I have seen the beautiful way that they love the people God brings across their paths and the nations that He takes them to, from orphaned children and distributing bibles to African church leaders to seats of governmental powers and heads of states. I have witnessed their tenacity as they have stood for justice and peace in their community. I have seen the gracious way they have come alongside others with stories of hope and encouragement and prophetic wisdom. I have stood with them as they have laughed and watched the hand of God do spontaneous miracles before their very eyes.

And I have been inspired!

Even as you turn the pages of this book, you can feel the confirmation of the Holy Spirit in each story - directing your heart to praise the God who will let us partner with Him as He releases the destiny of the nations.

And so, I urge you to be expectant as you read this book. As you read, to let these stories ignite in you a passion to partner with God for the transformation of your family, community, city and nation.

And to open your life before the God who wants to take you by the hand and lead you on the greatest adventure you have ever known.

The faith, the love, the hope, the presence of God and the adventure is the lifestyle of my dear friend Sue Sinclair.

Welcome to the adventure!

Bishop Arnold Muwonge
Founder and Executive Director
NDE Network and Kampala Children's Centre

LET THE ADVENTURES BEGIN....

When I signed up to give my life to Jesus I did not sign up to simply sit in a pew on a Sunday morning. I signed up for an exciting relationship with the living God. I started by hungrily devouring the pages of the New Testament reading the stories of the birth of the Church with great interest. Life for the disciples was never dull or boring and it was not long before I realised that mine was not going to be either.

In the Cambridge Dictionary - Adventure is defined as "an unusual, exciting and possibly dangerous activity, such as a trip or an experience."

Helen Keller said, "Life is either a daring adventure or nothing at all".

From walking through the White House in Washington DC to walking with lions in South Africa, I guess I can say that life has certainly not been without adventures for me either!

I soon discovered that most of the Bible is actually packed full of stories of unusual, exciting and definitely dangerous activities, trips and experiences. A great example of this is the account in Daniel 3 where you can read the scary story of three friends Shadrach, Meshach and Abednego. These men defied the laws of the land and were thrown into a furnace, so hot that the flames of the fire killed the soldiers who prepared it. However, Shadrach, Meshach and Abednego came out alive without even the smell of fire upon them because they were obedient to God and confident that He would save them.

God can do so much without our assistance but for some reason beyond our comprehension, He chooses to partner with us to bring about His purposes. He usually prefers the weak and the foolish and makes His strength and wisdom available to us, so that He gets the glory.

Another incredible story is found in Jonah Chapters 1 and 2. It relates to the tale of Jonah, who ran away from the assignment God had called him to. Instead of going to Nineveh, he chose to board a ship. As a result of his disobedience Jonah found himself in a dangerous storm, endangering not only his life but also the lives of those on board. Eventually, to save the lives of everyone else on the ship, Jonah was thrown overboard. However, God had not finished with Jonah and gave him another rather bizarre opportunity, by sending a whale to swallow him. Wow, that is a very dangerous adventure that I really do not want to go on!

I have learned the importance of listening to God and being obedient no matter what the facts look like or how silly the start of the journey may appear. The good news is that throughout all of our adventures I have not been swallowed by a whale yet, although I have wondered what the inside of a whale really looks like! However, I have been in a vehicle that was charged by an angry bull elephant in Uganda, I wonder if that counts as unusual and dangerous?

I have learned that having a relationship with Jesus is not about being religious, but it is about being a part of an exciting life-giving relationship. Jesus often invites me into completely impossible situations. After all, if He asks me to do things I can do easily, then He would not get the glory.

I have learnt that if Jesus calls me to do something He always provides, always empowers and always knows where He is leading me. No matter how things appear at the beginning of the journey I can always trust God 100%.

"I know your deeds. See, I have placed before you an open door that no one can shut. I know that you have little strength, yet you have kept My word and have not denied My name." Revelation 3:8

It has been my experience that when you obey God and do not deny Him, He opens the most incredible and unbelievable doors. To be honest with you, I have been astounded at the places I have found myself in and although I have often felt totally inadequate, my experience has shown that with God all things are possible.

I love these verses of scripture that have certainly proved to be true in my life:

"I can do all things through Christ who strengthens me." Philippians 4:13

"With God all things are possible." Matthew 19:26

God is limitless, so what we can do through His love, power, and strength has no limits either! When God calls us to go somewhere or to do something we have access to everything we need to succeed. Actually we have the same power that raised Jesus from the dead available to us. Yes available to us!

I love these verses written by the Apostle Paul from Ephesians 3:16-20:

"I pray that out of his glorious riches he may strengthen you with power through his Spirit in your inner being, so that Christ may dwell in your hearts through faith. And I pray that you, being rooted and established

in love, may have power, together with all the Lord's holy people, to grasp how wide and long and high and deep is the love of Christ, and to know this love that surpasses knowledge - that you may be filled to the measure of all the fullness of God.

Now to him who is able to do immeasurably more than all we ask or imagine, according to his power that is at work within us, to him be glory in the church and in Christ Jesus throughout all generations."

I love that! God wants to do immeasurably more than we can ask or imagine. This means that Father God created us with the potential to carry His presence and to do things so large, extensive and extreme, it is impossible to measure. Why then do we settle for so much less? If that were not enough, we have God's word and His promises. We have access to all the resources of heaven, so let us be sure to utilise them.

In my first book "Extravagant Fire" I explained the foundations that have been laid in my life and the preparations for the "Extravagant Adventures" God has in store for me. You will also find that God has been working extensively throughout your life preparing you for the adventures He has in store for you. Choose life with Jesus, take hold of the keys God has for you and choose to be an Adventurer!

THE KEYS TO BREAKTHROUGH

I have learned that to be an adventurer you need to take hold of the keys that God has for you to breakthrough personally and for you to bring breakthrough for others. The keys to breakthrough are really simple. So simple in fact that most of the time we miss them completely!

It is important that we understand:

1) Who God is;
2) Who we are;
3) How to connect with God.

Then we can be vessels to release heaven to earth.

UNDERSTANDING WHO GOD IS

When we are born we usually receive our Father's family name and we become an heir to all that our earthly Father owns. However, when we become a Christian we begin a relationship with our heavenly Father and we take on the name of Christ. We are adopted into King Jesus' family and we become an heir of the King with full access to all of His resources.

When we understand this we can draw on the name and resources of Jesus. Whatever your family name, the name of Jesus Christ is more powerful and is the name above every other name – Philippians 2:9.

The Lord's Prayer says we should hallow God's name and if we take on the name of Christ what does that mean? How do we do that?

I have learnt that God's names, His acts, and His glory are all inseparable. His names describe who He is, what He has done in the past, what He is doing and what He will do in the ages to come.

I suggest that you spend some time exploring the names of God in the Bible. Here are just a few of God's names that have proved to be true for me:

- Jehovah-Jireh = Our provider.
Genesis 22:13-14. God has ALWAYS provided for us as a family and throughout my years in ministry. In the past I have experienced God as my provider when He broke poverty off our lives, released His blessings and taught us that when you come to the end of your resources, God releases His supply.

- Jehovah-Elohim = God of power.
Psalm 19:1. God has moved in incredible ways, changing nations through a whispered prayer.

- Jehovah-Shalom = Our peace.
Judges 6:24. God has often released His Shalom peace in my life despite our circumstances enabling us to walk through to the other side of the pain.

- Jehovah-Rophe = Our healer.
Exodus 15:26. God has healed me several times and healed many people through our ministry. The most exciting miracles have

happened when I have felt the weakest. Jesus healed my back when I was in so much pain I was struggling to walk, sit or lie down. Jesus simply touched my back and it was instantly healed. Another time He performed several miracles during my pregnancy, saving my little baby in the womb when so many things were wrong.

- Jehovah-Sabbaoth = The Lord of Hosts.

Isaiah 6:1-3. You can read the story of what God did as the Lord of Hosts when we visited Uganda for the first time later on in this book.

- Jehovah-Nissi = A banner of love and protection.

Exodus 17:15-16. He has always, always been there for me as my heavenly Father who loves me with a passion.

- Jehovah-Shammah = God is with us.

Ezekiel 48:35. God is "Emmanuel", which means God with us, every day of the year and not just at Christmas.

"The people who know their God will display strength and take action." Daniel 11:32

As we start to understand who God is, we can claim our full inheritance and believe that if God lives in us, then we have all those qualities available to us.

When we live our lives knowing who God really is, we can be very confident in doing what God created us for and calls us to do. It has certainly been true in my life, as God has provided everything He thinks I need to fulfil my destiny.

We are made to be like God, to be His Ambassadors and representatives here on earth. We can only do that when we have all the resources of heaven available to us. God created us to be vessels to bring heaven to earth, to transform and change the land we live in.

From the beginning of eternity we were on God's heart and He knew exactly when and where we would be born. No matter what the circumstances, we were born on time and in the right place for God's plan. For He has a destiny and a purpose for our lives that nobody else can fulfil. We need to believe that, as we are the only ones who can take a hold of it.

We need to discover how God speaks to us and what gifts He has given to us. How does God speak to you? Here are a few ways that God speaks but there are many more:

1) Through His Word
2) Through nature - Romans 1:20
3) Through other people.
4) Through music.
5) Through circumstances.
6) Through the Holy Spirit.
7) Through prayer - Romans 8:26-27
8) Through dreams - personally this is one of the ways that God speaks to me.
9) Through visions
10) Through His voice

When we understand this or even when we are en-route to discovering this, we are ready for God to use us to bring heaven to earth. If you want to see a breakthrough that not only changes your life, but also impacts your community and your nation, you need to understand who God is, who you are and how to release heaven to earth.

For me, living in Liverpool has been an amazing journey of discovery. Firstly I fell in love with my city as God showed me how much He loves Liverpool and the precious people who live here. Now I love Liverpool with a passion and I meet with others who are equally as passionate!

In 2002 we watched the Transformation Videos from The Sentinal Group produced by George Otis Jnr. and Rev. Dr. Alistair Petrie[1]

These videos profoundly impacted me, and many others who watched them. The videos spelled out what happened when God's people began to pray together and seek His face to see their communities transformed by God's love and power. The first story I watched many times and wept every time, as I witnessed the physical and spiritual transformation of Cali in Columbia. Cali was a town ravaged by gangs, drug and alcohol addiction, daily murders, crime, violence and family breakdown.

One of the Pastors, Holio Ruibal had been struggling to bring the Church Leaders together to pray, was gunned down and killed. The shocked Church Leaders came together and cried out to God in desperation and repentance, with an understanding of the issues of their land. They gathered the Church in unity and multitudes came to worship and pray. Within days Cali began to change as the murders stopped and lives began to be radically transformed. Gang leaders gave their lives to Jesus and many lives were changed by God's power and love.

Another video told the story of Almolonga, Guatemala where many in the town had been involved in idol worship. Most of the men had become alcoholics who were incapable of standing most of the time, let alone completing a full days work. As a result of this the land suffered and the crops failed for the lack of good farming practises. Once again when God's people began to pray, men began to repent and give their lives to God. As they did many of them were set free from their addictions. Their working patterns changed dramatically and so did their harvests. The land suddenly began to produce giant vegetables with a thousand percent increase in agricultural productivity.

I was so inspired by these stories, but I knew that the physical transformation of Liverpool, that we desired and God desires, was never going to look like big carrots and cabbages!

Since that time, as we have prayed and prophesied (declared God's word) to our very broken city, we have watched it transform before our very eyes. God has taught us so much that we have put into practise elsewhere and taught to others. We are watching as God is using His people to bring transformation to their communities and cities.

I would like to share my story with you and I hope that it helps to inspire you in your journey.

1 Available from http://revivalworks.com/dvds/documentary-dvds

LIVERPOOL
A ROYAL GATEWAY

It is helpful for us to understand some of the relevant history of our communities. For we stand on the foundations that those who gave gone before us have laid and our children, grandchildren and great grandchildren will stand on the foundations that we lay in our lifetime. This is some of Liverpool's amazing story and I share this as an example of how God can move so powerfully, as we simply stand in the gap and use the keys God has given to us to bring breakthrough. The change comes, when we understand which are the doors to the past that are withholding the blessing, how they can be locked up and which doors can release the blessings, for the present and the future. As you read Liverpool's story I suggest that you ask God about your community.

King John created the free borough of Liverpool via a charter in 1207. Prior to this, Liverpool was just a little fishing village with livestock markets, serving the immediate area with a small population of less than two thousand people. Liverpool grew very rapidly over the following years, mainly as a result of the Slave Trade. By 2013 it had a population of 466,400 and the wider area of Merseyside had a population of approximately 1.38 million.

Like many large cities Liverpool has a very varied history and is known throughout the world for pioneering many amazing things. You may not know it but the city actually has a gift for restoring life, in so many ways.

The Liverpool School of Tropical Medicine was founded in 1898 and received the Nobel Prize for Medicine, for discovering that malaria is caused by mosquito bites. (I do wonder why God created mosquitoes?) Today in the Liverpool School of Tropical Medicine they are successfully pioneering a vaccine, that we hope will eventually help to eradicate malaria. Having a friend in Uganda whose beautiful two-year old daughter died from malaria, I will be very pleased to see that vaccine available to everybody.

Here are just a few more of the life changing and amazing things that have been pioneered, in Liverpool by its people.

1791 - The first school for the blind opened.

1793 - Liverpool became the first and only municipality with the right to issue its own money! Sadly this is no longer functioning!

1825 - World's first school for deaf people was opened.

1830 - World's first inter-city passenger railway line was launched, although the celebrations for the launch were marred when William Huskisson MP was run over and killed by the Rocket locomotive engine.

1883 - The Liverpool Society for the Prevention of Cruelty to Children (NSPCC) was founded.

1891 - John Brodie invented goal nets first used in Goodison Park, the home of Everton FC also the world's first purpose built football ground. No wonder we are football crazy in Liverpool!

1894 - The first ever radio broadcast was made by Oliver Lodge, Liverpool University Professor of Physics.

1896 - The x-ray was first used in medical diagnosis.

Prince Albert in 1846 said, "I have heard of the greatness of Liverpool but the reality far surpasses the expectation."

Sadly Liverpool also has a reputation for some dreadful things too including bloodshed and death, as a result of the international Slave Trade. Liverpool actively supported the Confederates in the American Civil War both physically and financially in order to maintain the trade as long as possible. In fact the City of Liverpool supported the Confederates so much that there was even a Confederate Embassy in Liverpool. A little known fact is that at the end of the war, the last Confederate surrender occurred on 6th November 1865, when the warship CSS Shenandoah surrendered in Liverpool. Captain James Bulloch remained in Liverpool and was buried in the Toxteth Cemetery.

Liverpool is also known for its involvement with the Irish potato famine, when multitudes of starving people crossed over the Irish Sea to start their voyage on their way to America. Many people came to Liverpool in those days from all over the UK and Europe to make their voyage to America. Thankfully many families who came loved Liverpool so much that they actually stayed and contributed to our wonderful multicultural community. However, with such a large Irish population, Liverpool experienced some bitter divisions between the Catholic and Protestant communities. Thankfully much of this has now been resolved, as the Church is leading the way to reconciliation; through the work started by the Bishop of Liverpool David Sheppard and Archbishop Derek Worlock. To honour their ministry, a beautiful 15 foot/4.5 metre bronze statue of the two men, has been erected halfway along Hope Street, which is the road that connects Liverpool's two cathedrals.

Liverpool has a significant and varied maritime history too, particularly its involvement as the major Royal Navy and Merchant Navy Port during the two World Wars. It was so strategic during World War II that it was the home of Western Approaches, the War Room for all that occurred upon the seas. As a consequence of that Liverpool became a major target for the Germans, resulting in it being bombed on 79 occasions. It paid a very high price, suffering a huge loss of life with 2,596 men, women and children killed and many more injured. Bodies lay in the street and were buried under the enormous piles of rubble. There was massive destruction, with over 11,000 homes destroyed and over 150,000 badly damaged. Many businesses were also destroyed and it took decades to recover.

Despite the battering it took, Liverpool played a powerful role in the war and still managed to handle over 85,000 tons of cargo and remained the main national port of entry for essential supplies. In 1941 Prime Minister Winston Churchill, said about Liverpool, "I see the damage done by the enemy attacks, but I also see the spirit of the people."

There is a great sound that comes from Liverpool that has manifested in many different ways over the years, particularly during the 1950's and 1960's. Did you know that there have been more number one chart successes that have come from Liverpool than any other city in the world? The most famous of course would be the Beatles whose song ALL YOU NEED IS LOVE became No 1 both in the UK and USA. This song was actually commissioned by the BBC for the first live global television link on "Our World". Watched by over 150 million in 26 countries, the programme was broadcast on 25th June 1967.

The Beatles were asked to come up with a song with a message that would be understood by everyone. Brian Epstein said, "It was an inspired song and they really wanted to give the world a message. The nice thing about it is that it cannot be misinterpreted. It is a clear message saying that love is everything." What a great sound and message that needs to go around the world once again.

Our city has had seasons of dynamic success, particularly with its popular football teams Liverpool and Everton. Wherever you go in the world people have heard of Liverpool Football Club because of their European, league and FA cup successes.

Liverpool has experienced times of desperate shame and pain too, including the Heysel and Hillsborough disasters, both connected with football games.

However, God created the people of Liverpool with boldness and courage to overcome and to laugh through their pain. This is something that has been needed when we have gone through so much adversity. We have wept together, laughed together and overcome together. No doubt we will continue to do that.

Liverpool is a place of great diversity and we stand on the shoulders of the giants who have gone before us. We thank God for the entrepreneurs and pioneers, who filled with compassion could not ignore those in need and as a result started charities that transformed the lives of the poor, the vulnerable and the broken.

We were privileged to have spiritual giants visit our region, with Evan Roberts coming to Bootle, Liverpool and Birkenhead in April 1905. Then in 1926, George Jeffreys visited Liverpool to hold several missions, leaving a powerful spiritual legacy following a massive outpouring of revival power. I would love to have experienced that. This is a report from his visit:

> "Revival Fires are burning in Liverpool. Although the campaign only started on Sunday 14th March, by the middle of the week the church was packed out. Hundreds have been saved and there have been many remarkable healings."

There have been many times of spiritual breakthrough in Liverpool and there have also been plenty of other breakthroughs too.

Liverpool is an extraordinary gateway place that even today leads to many regions of the world. That is why it is such an important place spiritually. What happens here affects the places it leads to, for good or evil. Liverpool as a city and a community of people was created to bring breakthrough, not just for us but also for the nation and nations. When we are filled with the Holy Spirit we can be used by God to bring healing, deliverance, miraculous financial provision and new business ideas that can be released across the world.

As we love people and our communities the way that God does, we can be used by God, to bring to earth all the vision and creativity that is stored up in heaven. When ordinary people put their lives in the hand of an extraordinary God anything can happen, and for us it often does.

We have learned to understand ourselves - that we were made by God in His image to have dominion and authority within our communities and nations. We have learned to understand what we carry in our DNA as people from Liverpool, a royal gateway place. We are gateway people who have authority to open up our gateway for good to come in or go out, and we have the authority to shut the gates to keep evil out. We are creative people who, with the help of the Holy Spirit, can speak things into being to see lives and communities transformed.

> *"I will clothe him with your robe and fasten your sash around him and hand your authority over to him. He will be a father to those who live in Jerusalem and to the people of Judah. I will place on his shoulder the key to the house of David; what he opens no one can shut, and what he shuts no one can open. I will drive him like a peg into a firm place; he will become a seat of honour for the house of his father. All the glory of his family will hang on him: its offspring and offshoots."* Isaiah 22:21-24

As we understand who we are and we follow the lead of the Holy Spirit, life becomes the most amazing adventure and you never know what may happen.

The disciples asked Jesus to teach them how to pray and this is the prayer:

Our Father in heaven,
Hallowed be your name,
Your kingdom come,
Your will be done,
On earth as in heaven.
Give us today our daily bread.
Forgive us our sins
As we forgive those who sin against us.
Lead us not into temptation
But deliver us from evil.
For the kingdom,
The power,
And the glory are yours
Now and forever. Amen.

This is known as the Lord's Prayer, and it is clear that we are to be agents of God to bring His Kingdom from heaven to earth. This is not just an empty prayer, this is a possibility when you position yourself to be used by God.

Here are just some of the stories from our adventures with CWM (our team) that interweave with the story of Liverpool. It is not for us to boast about ourselves but to encourage you. I would also add that over the years many people have been praying behind the scenes and we also want to honour them for their faithfulness.

As we have played our part, God has moved very powerfully. We have been amazed at what has happened, not only in Liverpool but in every place that God has led us to. If God can use us to touch communities, governments and nations, the good news is that He can use you too.

What does God have planned for your community, city or nation? How does He want to use you to bring that change?

Paving the Way
for Breakthrough

One of my favourite passages of scripture is from Isaiah 61:1-4:

> *"The Spirit of the Sovereign Lord is upon me, because the Lord has anointed me to proclaim good news to the poor. He has sent me to bind up the brokenhearted, to proclaim freedom for the captives and release from darkness for the prisoners, to proclaim the year of the Lord's favor and the day of vengeance of our God, to comfort all who mourn, and provide for those who grieve in Zion - to bestow on them a crown of beauty instead of ashes, the oil of joy instead of mourning, and a garment of praise instead of a spirit of despair. They will be called oaks of righteousness, a planting of the Lord for the display of his splendor. They will rebuild the ancient ruins and restore the places long devastated; they will renew the ruined cities that have been devastated for generations."*

This not only speaks of Jesus but it speaks of us – the Spirit of the Sovereign Lord is upon us, as we carry His presence, He anoints us to proclaim the good news to the poor. We are anointed to be agents of change and transformation for the lives of those around us and for our communities.

As I look back over the years, I can see how God led our CWM team step by step. We certainly did not see the whole path ahead of us, but we have simply learnt to trust God for one step at a time, that was usually the only step we could see.

To be honest, most of the time we did not know what we were doing. We did not learnt from a seven-step program in a book or DVD. We simply allowed the Lord to lead us, and our first steps began with clearing away the old so that the new could begin to arise.

The journey always starts with us and I found the analogy given in my first book "Extravagant Fire" of the controlled burning used to destroy everything that hinders new life, a good one. I recommend you read that for greater understanding. Personally this helped me to understand who I really was and not who other people wanted me to be. We are always a work in progress, and this helped me to deal with the rubbish in my life that kept me as a victim of my past, so that I could run the race God created me for. Having done that as a team we were then led to begin to understand what was hindering Liverpool's growth.

The first and most significant thing that the Lord brought to our attention was Liverpool's massive and shocking link with the Transatlantic Slave Trade. By the middle of the 18th century, ninety-five percent of all slave voyages took place from one of Britain's three major ports, Liverpool, London and Bristol. Liverpool benefited financially in at least five major ways:

- By the building and repair of slave ships.
- Through the trading of 1.5 million slaves.
- Through goods produced - cotton and sugar.
- By producing goods to exchange for slaves.
- By insuring and financing the industry.[1]

It was not only Liverpool who bought into and benefited from the slave trade, in fact most of the nation invested and profited from it. However it was our responsibility to deal with Liverpool's role.

THE LIVERPOOL LEGACY

During the period of the slave trade, ships sailed from Liverpool to West Africa. There, they picked up men, women and children, and took them under inhumane conditions to the islands of the Caribbean and the southern states of North America, where they were sold as slaves. The ships emptied of their cargo then returned home, laden with sugar, cotton and rum. The ships and their valuable cargos made their owners very rich. Evidence of this can be seen by the many magnificent buildings across Liverpool still surviving from those days.

By the middle of the 18th century Liverpool employed more than half of the ships involved in the Transatlantic Slave Trade, and they were responsible for taking more than half of the slaves exported by all ships in Britain. A large part of this profit was returned to a small number of prominent Liverpool men who held both political and economic power. Liverpool arguably is the city in Britain that was most complicit in the slave trade.

By 1750, ten of Liverpool's fourteen most prominent banks were owned by slave traders. In 1787, thirty seven out of the forty one members of the Liverpool Council were involved in some way in slavery and all of Liverpool's twenty Lord Mayors, who held office between 1787 and 1807, were involved.

"Amazing grace, how sweet the sound" are the words at the beginning of one of my favourite hymns. John Newton, the writer of this famous hymn was actually a Captain of a slave vessel that sailed on these despicable journeys in and out of Liverpool. Newton's mother had taught him about Jesus, but he had walked away from God. However, as a storm arose on a homeward voyage, he experienced what he later referred to as his "great deliverance" as God saved them all. From 1755 to 1760 Newton was surveyor of tides at Liverpool, where he met and was impacted by the ministry of George Whitefield and John Wesley.

John Newton became a Church of England minister in London where he drew large congregations. Newton influenced many, among them William Wilberforce, who one day became a leader in the campaign for the abolition of slavery. John Newton came full circle.

HEALING THE PAST, BUILDING THE FUTURE

For many years since then Christians in Liverpool cried out to God in repentance for what had happened during the Slave Trade years. Our little team came in at the end of that season, thanking God for all those who had prayed before us. We continued to pray through until a powerful turning point came for Liverpool on 9th December 1999. As a final act of the Millennium, Liverpool City Council unanimously passed a motion apologising for the city's role in the Slave Trade, linked to a commitment to policies that would end racism and work to create a community where all were equally valued:

> "Liverpool City Council expresses its shame and remorse for the city's role in this trade in human misery. The City Council makes an unreserved apology for Liverpool's involvement in the Slave Trade and its continued effects on the city's Black Communities. The City Council hereby commits itself to work closely with all Liverpool's communities and partners and with the peoples of those countries which have carried the burden of the slave trade."

We see it as a fruit of all of this prayer that the "Reconciliation Triangle" was set up under the motto, "Healing the Past Building the Future." This project was led by Lord David Alton of Liverpool, "designed to confront the legacies of slavery in Africa, the Americas and Europe, and to heal the wounds of society."

In 2004, Liverpool became one of the first cities in Europe to make International Slavery Remembrance Day an official part of its cultural calendar. It formally adopting 23rd August as the International Day for the Slave Trade and its Abolition as an annual civic occasion for the city.

The Reconciliation Triangle now links the cities of Liverpool and Richmond, Virginia with the West African Republic of Benin. The aim of this initiative is to foster:

- historical understanding:
- conflict resolution:
- reconciliation and justice;
- healing;
- the promotion of the cultural heritage;
- socio-economic development.

As part of this project, artist Stephen Broadbent created a beautiful sculpture of reconciliation - two figures are closely entwined, he called it "Embrace". Three copies of this statue were made, each 4.06 meters high. An inscription on the base of the sculpture says, "Acknowledge the past, embrace the present, shape a future of reconciliation and justice." I love those life-shaping words.

One was shipped over to Virginia USA where it was installed in the former slave market, the place where 300,000 kidnapped Africans and their descendants had been sold. The second was installed in Benin, Africa, the place where the slaves were taken and thrown into the cramped holds of slave ships. The Ambassador of Benin called it "a blessed completion." The third and final one can be found in Bold Street, Liverpool.

SOWING LIFE

During the summer of 2005, the Lord spoke to Community Watchmen Ministries (CWM). He said, *"Liverpool no longer needs to repent of her past regarding the slave trade. Liverpool is now walking in the forgiveness and blessing of God, however we now need to sow life into Africa."*

Since then, we have worked hard with many partners, raising over £112,000 to build Abundant House and New Beginnings House as part of the Kampala Children's Centre[2]

They are homes to precious children orphaned by HIV, AIDS and the activities of the Lord's Resistance Army in the North of Uganda. We are hoping to build another home in the next few years to change the future of another twelve children. We have visited Kampala Children's Centre over many years and continue to partner with them.

We have also been honoured to work with thousands of Church Leaders from Uganda, Burundi, Kenya, Congo and many other East African nations. We have provided Bibles and materials to communities that did not have access to God's Word.

In July 2006, during our visit to Washington DC, we took the opportunity to apologise for Liverpool's support of the Confederate Army during the American Civil War. After all thirty-five vessels were constructed in Merseyside docks, including the notorious raider CSS Alabama.

After the repentance declaration from Liverpool, we began to see the curse that we believe came from our involvement in slavery lifting from the land, and the blessing of God starting to be released very powerfully. We give God the glory for all that has happened and we look to Him for completion of what has begun.

1 http://www.liverpoolmuseums.org.uk/ism/slavery/europe/liverpool.aspx

2 http://www.kampalachildren.com

HEYSEL STADIUM

People from Liverpool are passionate about all kinds of things, including sport, and particularly football. We usually demonstrate that through our two main football teams - Liverpool and Everton. People are usually red or blue! Over the years both football clubs have seen incredible success and humiliating failures. No matter whether they succeed or fail the passion does not diminish.

During the 1980's there was great unrest amongst many football fans internationally. Shamefully, this often led to riots and people being hurt throughout Britain and Europe. The people involved were not considered to be true football fans but people who were often there just to pick a fight. It was a well known fact that there were gangs who were not even particularly attached to a football club, but attended matches with no other focus than to start trouble.

By 1984 Liverpool FC was established as the premier football team in Europe and they had won the European Cup for a fourth time. That year they had played A.S.Roma in Rome and despite being escorted by the Italian police, the buses containing the Liverpool fans, were attacked with bricks and several Liverpool fans were stabbed. The following year, 1985, Liverpool FC had continued their success in the competition and had reached the final again. They were the defending champions of Europe and once again they faced Italian opposition with Juventus.

In every disaster there are usually many contributing factors and the Heysel Stadium disaster was no different. The Heysel Stadium, despite being the national Belgium Stadium, located in Brussels, was unsuitable for such a prestigious match. The management of Liverpool FC led by Manager Joe Fagan raised their concerns regarding the safety, weeks prior to the match. However UEFA insisted that the game should be played there as planned.

Unfortunately, one of those factors on the 29th May 1985 was that the Police were not positioned appropriately within the ground and their radios were not functioning effectively. To add to this problem, a friend of mine, who was there, said there was an issue with black market tickets and badly managed turnstile entrances. She told me that people were simply bundled through the entrances without many tickets being checked and fans on the troubled terrace were segregated by mere chicken wire. There were volatile exchanges with individuals intimidating each other, making offensive gestures and chants long before the actual explosion into violence. Despite the Italian fans wearing scarves to cover their faces and running toward the Liverpool fans, threatening them with weapons, the police did nothing. Even with the bad behaviour of the fans, had the Police been effective, the disaster may have been averted.

Prior to this match Liverpool FC had maintained an excellent reputation and were not known for fighting and rioting. However, when the Juventus fans began to throw objects and threaten the Liverpool fans, the Liverpool fans reacted inexcusably. They charged across the terraces at the Juventus fans, who were not safely segregated within the ground. Fighting broke out causing the Juventus fans to retreat. Having no way out, the Juventus fans ran towards the side perimeter wall and some managed to climb over and escape. However the wall was not safe and could not withstand the force of the fleeing Italian supporters. The wall collapsed causing the death of 39 people and injuring a further 600 people.

Football should be a game where people chase a ball around a piece of grass and each team aims to score in the opposition goal, without conceding any goals themselves. Surely it should be that simple? It should not be a sport where people on the pitch or in the terraces, fight, get injured or even, at the worst, lose their lives. In the history of football this was one of the worst days. This was not sport and those people who committed this horrendous atrocity were not true football fans. The general population of Liverpool were ashamed, appalled and disgusted.

The British police undertook a thorough investigation to ensure those who were guilty were brought to justice. People were arrested on suspicion of manslaughter, which was the only extraditable offence applicable to events at the Heysel Stadium. In 1989, the men returned to Brussels for their trial and some of them were accommodated by a Christian couple. After a five-month trial, fourteen Liverpool fans were given three-year sentences for involuntary manslaughter.

Some good news in the midst of that horrific, disgraceful saga was that some of the men gave their lives to Jesus before they went into prison and some did whilst in prison. After being released from prison one man returned to the Heysel Stadium to apologise and has walked with Jesus ever since.

Back in the United Kingdom the British Prime Minister at the time, Margaret Thatcher, was furious and determined to solve the problem of rioting football fans. Despite the overspill of fans on to the pitches on several occasions previously to avoid crushing, a decision was made to fence the fans into pens in all stadia across the UK. There would certainly be no further opportunities for fans to riot or invade the pitches. Sadly, as you will see in the next chapter this decision was to prove extremely fatal!

HILLSBOROUGH DISASTER

"You shall also be a crown of glory in the hand of the Lord and a royal diadem In the hand of your God. You shall no longer be termed Forsaken nor shall your land any more be termed Desolate; But you shall be called Hephzibah, and your land Beulah; For the Lord delights in you, and your land shall be married. For as a young man marries a virgin, so shall your sons marry you; and as the bridegroom rejoices over the bride, so shall your God rejoice over you." Isaiah 62:3-5.

When I fell in love and married Steve, I became very involved with His destiny. I care passionately about what happens to him and I really want to encourage him to fullfill his destiny. If He is blessed then I am blessed too! It is the same principal for our communities and cities.

"Work for the success of the city I have sent you to. Pray to the Lord for that city. If it succeeds, you too will enjoy success."
Jeremiah 29:7 (NIRV)

Being married to the land feels just like that. When you are "married to the land" and love it passionately, what happens to affect the land you care about and the people you love, touches your heart very deeply. I believe that it also really touches God's heart, as He loves the land because the people He loves live there and He created it. So I make no apologies for talking once again about football, as it affects the city of Liverpool and the people who live here very deeply. Football is not just about what happens with the teams on the pitch, but also how it impacts the lives of the supporters and their wider communities.

There are days in history that stick in your mind because of their significance. They stand out like milestones along the way and shape you for the future. These are the days that you look back at and you remember with great clarity where you were and what you were doing. The day that John Lennon or Princess Diana died were days like that. The 15th April 1989, almost four years after the Heysel disaster, was another one of those days that remains etched clearly in my memory.

Mum and I took my children out to a local community farm. It was a lovely sunny afternoon and the children loved looking at the goats and donkeys. At the back of my mind was the knowledge that Liverpool were playing Nottingham Forest in the FA Cup semi-final. This was one of the English football calendar's most significant days, with the prize of a trip to Wembley, then reserved only for Cup finals and England internationals. I looked at my watch several times wondering how the game was going.

Driving home the roads were deserted, as was always the case when Liverpool were playing a major game. If people were not at the match, they would normally be gathered around television sets watching it in local pubs or in their homes.

We got home a little while later and there was an eerie but tangible silence hanging in the air. I unlocked the front door and the children ran into the house excited to tell their Daddy all about the animals they had seen. However, Daddy was completely white with tears streaming down his face. "Have you heard the news?" Steve cried. "No, what has happened?" By now my eyes had gone to the television screen that Steve had been watching so intently. I could not believe my eyes, as I watched as lifeless bodies were being dragged out onto the football pitch. The commentators were clearly shocked at what was playing out before their eyes, as they were trying to get a clear grip of what was happening. They reported that they thought someone had died and tears began to pour down my cheeks as I thought of all the people who I knew would be at the match, including our neighbours and some of my work colleagues.

Over the minutes and hours that followed we were glued to the television screen as the tears continued to flow. This was in the days before mobile phones. We were desperate for news, but the news that came was not the news we wanted to hear. The death toll rose rapidly and it became clear very quickly that something really terrible had happened.

There were many lies told for too many years about what had happened on that day and the days that followed, but this is what we know about what happened. Liverpool FC should have been playing Nottingham Forest at the Hillsborough Stadium in Sheffield. The Liverpool fans as ever, were keen that victory would again be theirs. With the stakes so high, demand outstripped supply and tickets were scarce in both Nottingham and Liverpool.

Hillsborough Stadium was used regularly as a venue for the FA Cup semi-finals during the 1980s. As a result of Prime Minister Margaret Thatcher's instructions stadia were furnished with large metal fencing around the standing terraces to prevent the fans from rioting and spilling out on to the pitch. This would certainly be effective in stopping fans going on to the pitch when they should not, but it did not take into consideration how people could be evacuated if there was a problem in the terraces.

There had been a warning sign previously in 1981 when a crush had occurred in the Leppings Lane stand at the Hillsborough Stadium, causing thirty-eight injuries. This prompted Sheffield Wednesday to alter the design of the Leppings Lane end, and instead of the one supporters pen, they divided it into three separate smaller pens. Later again, they divided it into five even smaller pens when they were promoted to the First Division in 1984.

Liverpool and Nottingham Forest had also met at the semi-final stage of the same competition, at the same ground in the previous year. Many Liverpool fans including a friend of mine, reported crushing in the Leppings Lane end, leading to Liverpool FC lodging a complaint prior to the 1989 FA Cup semi-Final.

Hosting the semi-final game again at Hillsborough was controversial. The Liverpool FC management repeated their concerns that the club's larger number of supporters should be allocated the Spion Kop (a larger area) rather than the Leppings Lane end. Liverpool's unease was increased by the fact that the 24,256 capacity area designated for only twenty-three turnstile entrances, all located in the Leppings Lane area served the Liverpool fans. In contrast, the Forest fans had sixty turnstiles to enable them to enter the stadium safely.

Added to the background problems of policing the match, was the fact that Chief Superintendant Mole, who had supervised all of the police operations for the large matches played at the Hillsborough Stadium previously, was moved. Chief Superintendant David Duckenfield was brought in just a few weeks before to replace him. He had little time to familiarise himself with the issues involved, no understanding of the areas of potential hazard and 1,122 officers to supervise.

It was a beautiful sunny day as tens of thousands of fans made their way to Sheffield for a tie that promised to be one of the games of the season. Tragically, however, it is not the sunshine or the football that Saturday 15th April 1989 will always be remembered for. Instead it is remembered as the blackest day in British sport as ninety-six innocent men, women and children were crushed to death and many more were seriously injured and left traumatised.

On the day there was little supervision as the fans arrived at the Leppings Lane turnstiles and the crowd outside the stadium quickly increased. It was clear that people were in great danger of being crushed outside the stadium and, concerned that someone may die, Chief Superintendent David Duckenfield instructed Gate C to be opened. Suddenly many thousands of fans poured through the gates and most made their way into the tunnel immediately in front of them, not aware that the area was already packed full.

What followed was the worst ever football disaster in the history of English football. 90 men and 6 women died:

- 11 were less than 15 years old.
- 30 were between 16 and 20 years old.
- 90 people were less than 40 years old.
- The remaining 6 people were less than 70 years old.

All were in the prime of their lives - children, husbands, wives, fathers, mothers, brothers, sisters, friends, neighbours and colleagues; all had their life squeezed out of their bodies.

The match started on time, despite the problems outside the ground, but at 3.06pm the match was stopped. Bruce Grobbelaar, the Liverpool goalkeeper, who was shocked by what he could see unfolding, called to the referee Ray Lewis (my ex-boss from Berni Inn days) to stop the game.

It was a scene of complete chaos, as people were being crushed and others were trying to climb out over the fencing. Other fans were being rescued as fans from the top tier pulled them out from the crush. Whilst faces were turning from pink, to white, to blue as their bodies were being crushed against the fencing, all live on national television. Eventually some fans managed to get out of the enclosure, despite the police trying to push them back in again. The fans staggered out on to the pitch, some of them gasping for breath and collapsing. Whilst other fans struggled with all their strength to pull others out and to save lives. Many people survived that day because the fans themselves pulled them out from the crush and attempted their own emergency evacuation.

Whilst wrongly assuming that there was a riot going on, the Police initially refused to allow the emergency services into the stadium until it was far too late for many of the fans. Meanwhile the visible response by the majority of the police was to line up across the halfway line, fearing a public order problem rather than realising there was a life-threatening disaster unfolding. This was an ill judged and completely wrong assessment by the police leaders and as a result vital time was lost. Thankfully there were a few Police officers who used their initiative and we are thankful for them.

Major confusion occurred in the midst of the Police and emergency services, whilst innocent people were being crushed to death. Had the Police responded correctly and the emergency services been allowed onto the pitch, it is now a fact that many lives would have been saved.

If that was not bad enough, the families of those who died and the survivors then had to put up with the biggest smear campaign ever seen. This started within minutes, even as unconscious fans were being carried from the terrace. Chief Superintendent Duckenfield lied to cover his back (See Chapter 19) telling Football Association Chief Executive Graham Kelly that the crush had been caused by Liverpool fans forcing a gate open to gain admission. Graham Kelly then told this to a wider audience via the media.

That was, however, nothing compared to the allegations that appeared in The Sun newspaper a couple of days later. Below the now infamous headline

"The Truth", the newspaper carried allegations from unnamed police officers and 'sources' of how Liverpool fans had looted the bodies of the dead, urinated on police officers trying to help the injured, and even beaten up one officer while he was administering the kiss of life. All complete lies!

These lies, put together with what the families and the people of Liverpool, considered to be a distinct failure of anyone to be held accountable for what happened at Hillsborough, is why the sense of deep injustice burned fiercely for many years.

The deep pain in our city and region was horrific. Most people knew someone who had died or been injured. The hospitals were full of people with chest traumas and head injuries. Added to that we experienced journalists hovering on every street corner seeking out a story that supported their lies, which they never found. Survivors, who were actually heroes at Hillsborough by pulling people out from the crush and saving lives, now according to the media had become hooligans and thugs.

Liverpool is a unique place with unique people. We are like one big family that draws strength from one another during the times of great celebration and the times of trauma and heartache. This was one of those times when the people of Liverpool gathered to stand together shoulder to shoulder with the greatest dignity and humility to grieve. The Anfield Stadium, home of Liverpool FC, became the place where people assembled to pay their respects to those who had lost their lives. Fans from all around the world sent and brought football scarves as tributes and they were knotted together connecting the grounds of Everton FC and Liverpool FC through Stanley Park, a distance of about ¾ mile. My husband Steve and I queued silently for hours alongside thousands of people who had come to the Liverpool ground to place their tribute. There was little conversation but lots of tears.

Kenny Dalglish, the Liverpool Manager led the team in their incredible support of their fans. The funerals began and there were seventeen funerals just in my local community. Every funeral was attended by some of the players, who also spent time visiting the many fans still injured in hospital. The hope of many of the families was that the sound of the players' voices would cause their loved one to rally and awaken from their comas and some did.

I worked for Liverpool City Council at that time and I was transferred from the Architect's Department to work with the Mayor of Liverpool, Councillor Dorothy Gavin and others. We quickly opened up a small shop in the centre of Liverpool to create a space where people could come to talk or to donate to the Hillsborough Fund. Many people came, including survivors weighed down with guilt and not able to understand why they had survived whilst others all around them had died.

Shocked, traumatised and bewildered, the people of Liverpool and beyond believed that the truth of what happened at the Hillsborough disaster would be quickly revealed. We all assumed that the British justice system would prevail. However for many years a huge injustice was carried out as, to our horror, the truth was concealed time and time again. The Coroners Inquests recorded verdicts of accidental death, without even seeing the evidence or listening to relevant witnesses. The families of those who died and the survivors were badly treated. They were let down at every level as a huge cover up was mobilised that infected the Police, the emergency services, the justice system, the media and the government. How could this happen in our nation?

On the 8th May 1998 many Members of Parliament were present in the Houses of Parliament as they debated the Hillsborough Disaster once again, but despite their best efforts, there was no breakthrough.

RECEIVING THE COALS

In 2003, we heard that a friend of ours, Arnold Muwonge, was conducting a Prayer School in Helsby Methodist Church, hosted by Linda and Nick Holt. We decided to take a few of our team over to see how a Prayer School works, as we were planning to start our own Prayer School in the near future and we had a lot to learn.

Nick was very pleased, as they had just received a gift off a friend, Rowland Roderick from South Wales. It was almost the centenary of the Welsh Revival when Evan Roberts, himself an ex-miner, was used by God to bring many people to salvation. Rowland had sent a small bag of anthracite coal with a message to give some understanding of the price that was paid to mine it. It said, *"The anthracite coal burns very hot and was very costly to produce in those days, in fact a man died every 6 hours and men were injured every 2 minutes as they mined it from the pits of Wales"*. There was a short word of prophecy too, *"When we pray for God to send the fire, we need to understand that there is a cost. Just as Wales had been the land of revival fires, everywhere this coal will be taken God will send His revival fire."*

The Prayer School was great and at the end Arnold invited people to come forward if they wanted to receive a fresh touch from God. Arnold asked us to help minister, as so many people had responded. The Holy Spirit poured Himself out touching people in different ways with some on the floor, others laughing and giggling, some weeping and others just sitting quietly.

At the end of the session Nick asked me to close my eyes and put my hand out. I had no idea what he was about to do but trusted it was going to be something worthwhile. Nick placed something hard in my hand and as I opened my eyes I saw a beautiful piece of very shiny black anthracite coal. Instead of politely thanking Nick, I found myself asking for another piece, as I was hungry and desperate for the revival fires of God. To my amazement Nick walked away and returned moments later with three more pieces. Wow!!!!!

A few days later we met with the rest of the team and showed them the coal. We had four pieces of coal - just coal - nothing miraculous about it - nothing to be worshipped, just coal! Yet it was one of those incredible prophetic moments when God speaks and suddenly your whole life is thrown upside down or is it downside up?

God reminded us of the story of the talents from Matthew 25:14-30:

> *Again, it will be like a man going on a journey, who called his servants and entrusted his wealth to them. To one he gave five bags of gold, to another two bags, and to another one bag, each according to his ability. Then he went on his journey. The man who had received five bags of gold went at once and put his money to work and gained five bags more. So also, the one with two bags of gold gained two more. But the man who had received one bag went off, dug a hole in the ground and hid his master's money.*

> *After a long time the master of those servants returned and settled accounts with them. The man who had received five bags of gold brought the other five. "Master," he said, "you entrusted me with*

five bags of gold. See, I have gained five more." His master replied, "Well done, good and faithful servant! You have been faithful with a few things; I will put you in charge of many things. Come and share your master's happiness!"

The man with two bags of gold also came. "Master," he said, "you entrusted me with two bags of gold: see, I have gained two more." 'His master replied, "Well done, good and faithful servant! You have been faithful with a few things; I will put you in charge of many things. Come and share your master's happiness!"

'Then the man who had received one bag of gold came. "Master," he said, "I knew that you are a hard man, harvesting where you have not sown and gathering where you have not scattered seed. So I was afraid and went out and hid your gold in the ground. See, here is what belongs to you." 'His master replied, "You wicked, lazy servant! So you knew that I harvest where I have not sown and gather where I have not scattered seed? Well then, you should have put my money on deposit with the bankers, so that when I returned I would have received it back with interest. '"So take the bag of gold from him and give it to the one who has ten bags. For whoever has will be given more, and they will have abundance. Whoever does not have, even what they have will be taken from them. And throw that worthless servant outside, into the darkness, where there will be weeping and gnashing of teeth."

Just like the story of the talents we had a choice of what we would do with our pieces of coal. We could keep them all or we could give them to our friends. Maybe God had other ideas?

The Lord began to speak to us from Isaiah 6:
"In the year that King Uzziah died I saw the Lord sitting upon a throne, high and lifted up. And the skirts of His train filled the temple.

Above Him stood the seraphim: each had six wings; with two each covered his own face, with two covered his feet, and with two each flew. And one cried to another and said, "Holy, Holy, Holy is the Lord of Hosts; the whole earth is full of His glory. And the foundations of the threshold shook at the voice of him who cried, and the house was filled with smoke." Then said I, "Woe is me! For I am a man of unclean lips, and I dwell in the midst of people with unclean lips; for my eyes have seen the King, the Lord of Hosts!"

Then flew one of the seraphim to me, having a live coal in his hand which he had taken with tongs from off the altar and with it he touched my mouth and said "Behold this has touched your lips; your iniquity and guilt are taken and your sin is forgiven." And I heard the voice of the Lord saying, "Whom shall I send, who will go for us?" Then I said, "Here am I send me!"

Suddenly we sensed the holy presence of the Lord filling the whole room. We repented of everything we could repent of and asked God to cleanse our lips as we touched our lips with the coals. We told the Lord we would happily go wherever He wanted to send us. Little did we know what we had committed ourselves to! Before we had time to change our minds the Lord began to call us to take our pieces of coal to the nations.

God began to speak to us and tell us where each piece of coal was to be delivered. The first piece of coal was to stay in Liverpool for us to keep; that was easy! Then God clearly told us that the second was to go to Northern Ireland, but He did not tell us straight away where the other two should go? It would have been nice to give them to our friends; after all we would want them to receive the fire of God. However, unless we delivered them where God wanted them to go, when He wanted them to go there, nothing would happen.

I suddenly began to see the prophetic word that I had been given some years earlier in Cornwall, might actually come to pass after all.

God had said *"He was going to pour out a governmental anointing into my life and that He was going to take me to the nations. God was going to use me to speak and release His words into the lives of Prime Ministers, Kings and rulers. God was going to use me to change some of the governments and nations of the world."*

No wonder the Lord wanted me to be free of the fear of driving and travelling! Previously I had been crippled with a gripping fear just at the very thought of travelling anywhere. It rose up from the pit of my stomach and almost choked the life out of me. It literally terrified me to the point where I would be almost physically sick prior to travelling. I remember standing waiting at the bus stop with our children when it was freezing cold, windy and pouring with rain, while our car sat outside the house. When my Dad was dying of cancer in hospital a few miles away, I was desperate and I knew I needed to do something to overcome this fear.

I cried out to God for His help and then I took some steps to help myself. I asked God to clear the busy roads until I got my confidence and I got in the car and drove. I was so afraid as I gripped the steering wheel tightly, but the Lord went ahead of me and cleared the roads until my confidence was restored. Awesome God!

When my Dad was dying he received wonderful care from Marie Curie nurses at their Hospice in Woolton. Not long after he died, I was invited to participate in the Marie Curie Ladies Driving Challenge. This was a fundraising event but also a great opportunity to thank the Marie Curie for the priceless care they gave. So I signed myself up and set about raising as much sponsorship money as I could.

The day of the Driving Challenge came and it was really scary. However, I went along knowing that with God's help I had completely overcome the fear of driving and travelling. The first vehicle I stepped into was a bright red Mitsubishi Evo 6 and the driver smiled sweetly and strapped me into the passenger seat. I had no idea what I was letting myself in for! Moments later

I realised that my sweet driver was really a complete maniac as we were speeding around the racing track doing twists and turns at an incredible pace. I was screaming at the top of my lungs all the way around, much to the amusement of my driver!

I then had the opportunity to drive eight vehicles myself and to be marked with points out of ten for each one. The first one I drove was a lot more sedate, a huge green steamroller and I even got to wear the drivers' cap that went with it. It was hard work on the arms, as I had to turn a huge wheel to drive it but at least it gave me time for my legs to stop trembling after the Evo 6. Following this I drove a yellow tractor with 120 gears and completed all the maneuvers and lifts with a 9/10 mark.

Throughout the day I drove a brand new fire engine, a double-decker bus and a huge yellow CAT vehicle that was almost impossible to climb into. I drove an articulated lorry, completing reversing maneuvers successfully and I thoroughly enjoyed driving a tank complete with a huge gun. I will not tell you who I was imagining directing the gun towards! It was interesting driving a police response vehicle and being told by the Police Officer in the passenger seat to "put my foot down", even though it meant I would be breaking the speed limit.

There were a couple of other vehicles, before we got driven around in a couple of very classy cars. The men were only allowed to watch from the side and were certainly very envious. One man asked me with great interest, "Which cars have you been in?" I replied that I had been in a green one and a yellow one! Ladies you will understand the logic of this reply, while the men will be frustrated wanting to know what the car was and what size the engine was! I do remember one of them was a bright yellow Lotus Elise, which really impressed my son, as that was his dream car at the time.
Jesus set me free from the fears of driving and travelling, and now the pieces of coal needed to be delivered.

Smith Wigglesworth said *"Great faith is a product of great fights. Great testimonies are the outcome of great tests. Great triumphs can only come out of great trials".*

The world was beckoning and the adventures were about to begin!

NORTHERN IRELAND

Before we knew it, the trip to Northern Ireland was organised. Whilst praying a few days before the trip, the Lord spoke clearly to us and said that we needed to visit Stormont, the home of the Northern Ireland government.

I rang Barbara Brown, our wonderful host for the trip, and advised her of the Lord's instructions. Barbara spoke to David McClarty, a member of the Northern Ireland Assembly and David Trimble's Deputy. An election had been called for 26th November 2003 and once an election was called the members had to vacate the building so they did not have an unfair advantage. David volunteered to take us into Stormont the following Monday, which was the very last day he was permitted to go in until after the election.

On Monday 27th October Barbara took us to Stormont, where we were joined by Pat Smyrl and her daughter, Esther. David McClarty welcomed us and gave us an excellent guided tour of the chambers and other significant areas of the building. David told us that the Architect of Stormont was actually from Liverpool!

David led us into the Senate Chamber where we prayed for the main speakers. He then took us into the main chamber and explained where everyone sat and the way the chamber functioned. I sat in the Speakers seat and prayed for those who would sit there. We were shown where David Trimble, Gerry Adams, Martin McGuiness, the Rev Ian Paisley and all the main politicians all sat.

I asked David and he gave me permission to pray and proclaim the following scriptural declaration, which the Lord had given me the previous morning.

Therefore Stormont (Northern Ireland's Assembly) hear the word of the Lord. (Ezekiel 36:4)

I am calling you this day to set your house in order. To establish My authority throughout this land; To govern in justice and righteousness instead of fear and intimidation; To have a heart of compassion for this land and this people, instead of a heart for your own agendas and prejudices. (Isaiah 38:12)

I declare that violence shall no longer be heard in your land; neither wasting nor destruction within your borders; but you shall call your walls salvation and your gates praise. (Isaiah 60:18)

Thank you Lord that there is no authority except from you and the authorities that exist are appointed by you. (Romans 13:1)

Thank you Father that right now you are calling men and women to positions of authority in this government. Give them boldness and courage to stand in your fullness, to do and say the things you are calling them to do and say.

We call those with strategic roles to be placed in the correct positions; to hear the guidance of the Lord and to be obedient to that call of God upon your life. For you are called to government for such a time as this and we call upon you Lord for a sacred assembly to be established in this land.

We ask you Father for your Spirit to rest upon them; the Spirit of wisdom and understanding the Spirit of counsel and might; the Spirit of knowledge and the fear of the Lord. That their delight will be in the fear of the Lord and not religion. That they will not judge by the sight of their eyes nor decide simply by what they hear with their ears. But they will govern in righteousness and the fear of the Lord. (Isaiah 11:2)

For you alone Lord light our path and make our ways perfect. (Psalm 18:28)

We cry out to you Lord to visit this place and to restore the years that the locusts have eaten in this nation. To cause your rain to fall afresh upon this government, upon this nation and upon this land. We thank you for the former rains which brought revival fires of holiness and salvation. But Lord we ask you to send the wind of your Spirit to blow throughout this land again. (Joel 2:25)

We call upon the Church of this land to come together and we call upon the government of this land to come together. We call you to come together bone upon bone. We call upon the sinews and the flesh to come upon you. We call the breath of God to come from the North, the South, the East and the West. We call upon the body of the Church and the government of this nation to be filled with the fullness of the breath of God that you will live, that you will not die or be miscarried and you will fulfill God's destiny for you. We declare that this house shall be filled with men and women who will hear your voice and not those who will work against peace. (Ezekiel 37)

Pour out your Spirit Lord upon all flesh. (Psalm 39:7)

Answer the cries of your children in this nation, Father. Bring hope where there is hopelessness and despair for hope never disappoints. (Romans 5:5).

Bring peace where there is violence.

Father, we thank you that perfect love casts out all fear. We pray for your perfect love to fill this place and to anoint every seat, to touch every heart. We ask you Father, to cause faith to arise. We thank you that when our faith is in you we do not have a yoke of bondage to the world but we are free to serve you and to govern righteously. (1 John 4:18 & Galatians 5:6)

Show this government your ways, O Lord; teach them your paths.

Lead them in your truth and teach them. According to your mercy remember them. (Psalm 25:4)

I then presented David with the scriptures and the prayers we had used. We spent a couple of minutes praying for him and for each of the strategic leaders, before we were taken for lunch in the restaurant. David showed us the Long Room where President Bill Clinton was introduced to all the Members of the Legislative Assembly several years ago. We were honoured to be able to go into the Executive Room where the major decision-making process is usually carried out.

We were thrilled to have been escorted through Stormont by such a charming and courteous man. David was clearly placed in Stormont by God and we were really pleased to hear that he was returned to the Assembly after the election.

We prayed in the grounds, at a statue of Lord Edward Carson located in front of the executive building at Stormont. We spent some time in prayer about the signing of the notorious Ulster "blood" covenant on 28th September 1912. We declared the breaking of any curses and released blessings upon the nation. We declared the removal of the spirit of death off the nation and a new season of life to be released.

We then drove eighteen miles to Hillsborough Castle located outside of Belfast. This holds a unique place in the history of Northern Ireland, since it is the official royal residence and also the home of the Secretary of State for Northern Ireland. Actually, it is not a castle but a beautiful Georgian country house that has served as a venue for the formal and informal stages of the Peace Process. This includes the signing of the Anglo-Irish Agreement in 1985, the decommissioning talks in 1999, and the negotiation of the devolution of policing and justice powers in 2010 (known as The Hillsborough Agreement). Many of the informal negotiations leading up to the 'Good Friday' agreement were also held at Hillsborough.

We stood at the entrance of Hillsborough Castle and once again prayed for wisdom for those involved in the decision making process. We also anointed the gates for the King of Glory to be welcomed afresh into Northern Ireland. Being very security sensitive, cameras were mounted everywhere and followed our every movement. I am certain we kept somebody very amused as they watched us!

During our drive back into Belfast we drove past a vintage hearse being lifted onto a transporter truck. We believe the Lord was giving us a sign that death was being lifted off the land. I suggest that you always take time to look around after you have been praying, as the Lord often gives you an indication that He has heard your prayers and that something has shifted.

We presented our friends in Northern Ireland with a fire flag, along with our second piece of Welsh coal. We had a wonderful few days and a couple of evenings later the Lord gave us a spectacular light show in the heavens, as the Northern Lights (Aurora Borealis) shone immediately above Barbara's home. We gazed in awe and amazement as we thought we could see the face of Jesus appearing with a crown upon His head and the glory of God surrounding him. Moments later the sky changed and we could see an angel. The sky was filled with moving swirls of beautiful reds, greens, blues and yellows that lasted for a couple of hours. What a stunning sight and something we had always wanted to see. Again we felt this was a sign to us that God was shifting things in the heavens and soon we would witness the shift upon the earth.

We were privileged to travel to Northern Ireland, a nation where God's people have been praying for peace for many years. We honour those who have gone before us on their knees, crying out to God for the breakthrough to come. History now tells the story of the peace that has been restored since that time.

BRUSSELS

Back to the story of the pieces of coal - Ann Lewis, a precious member of the CWM team suggested that the third piece of coal should go to Brussels. Ann had previously lived in Brussels for fifteen years and so we took her suggestion very seriously. Despite this our diaries were very busy in 2004 and we could not see how our trip could happen before August 2005. As we all know though, God's ways and timings are not always the same as ours. However, suddenly and unexpectedly, the plans for our trip to Brussels fell into place.

Norma Dean from the CWM Team met a lovely lady called Brenda Ardern. Over a cup of tea Norma discovered that Brenda's cousin Liz and her husband Mike lived in Brussels. Mike worked for the European Commission and was also an Elder at the Brussels Vineyard Church, a vibrant congregation with over forty different nationalities. Before we knew it, we were introduced to Mike and Liz, and after praying together, the plans were put in place for our trip. During our time praying together, the Lord confirmed through Mike, that the destination for the fourth piece of coal was to be Washington DC.

It has to be said that the Holy Spirit Travel Agents is the best way to travel, as then the timing is always perfect! As we shared the vision for this trip Pauline

McGrory, Jean Dodd, Norma Dean, Pam Shaw, Ann Lewis, Debbie Edwards and Lynne Connolly all joined the team to go. So the preparations fell into place and from 17th to 22nd November we travelled to Brussels, Belgium and the surrounding area. We planned to visit the Heysel Stadium, Mons, Waterloo, the European Parliament and the Brussels Vineyard Church.

A week before we were due to go, we met to pray and Gary and Dawn Lacey decided to come with us. Gary was a red hot Liverpool supporter and had been at the Heysel Stadium at the time of the disaster. Gary described the scene, clearly still carrying the burden of witnessing the disaster. The Lord spoke to Gary and challenged him to sell his Kop season ticket for Liverpool FC and to come to Heysel with us – a sacrifice indeed!

We left Liverpool on Wednesday 17th November, which just happened to be the day of Emlyn Hughes's funeral in Sheffield (the home of the Hillsborough Stadium). Emlyn had played for Liverpool FC and was captain of the England football team for many years. Interestingly, Emlyn was actually present at both the Heysel Stadium disaster and Hillsborough disaster. Bill Bygroves, one of the Liverpool church leaders and Chaplain for Liverpool FC was preaching at the funeral. We knew that most of the Liverpool FC players and management both past and present would be there, including all those who would have been present in the team at the time of the Heysel disaster. Was this a God incidence?

HEYSEL STADIUM

Our flight to Brussels was excellent although it arrived an hour late, resulting in us arriving later than expected at the Heysel Stadium. We did not know it but there was an international match on with the Belgium team playing at 8.15pm, so the place was full of stewards and press etc. We walked around the whole perimeter of the stadium and all of the gates were locked. I was told that we would not be able to go in but I knew that if God wanted us to go in, He would make a way for us to get in. As it happened, we were perfectly on time, as we arrived at the last gate, just as three men were coming out of the VIP gate.

I approached the men and asked, "Excuse me but who are you?" I could not believe the courage and directness of my question, as I would not normally speak to people like that. The rest of the team hid behind me! The men explained that they were the management team of the Heysel Stadium - the very men we needed to speak to! Interestingly they did not speak good English, so it was helpful that I had spoken to them so directly.

We had not written, rung or emailed to ask for an appointment, we had simply prayed and trusted the Lord for a divine appointment. The Lord is so good at this! We spoke to them explaining that we had travelled from Liverpool to pray and to apologise for the behaviour of some of the Liverpool fans. Needless to say they were a little surprised, however they accepted our apology and found a steward to take us to the actual site where the wall had collapsed. It was very moving as we prayed prayers of repentance and asked for God's forgiveness and mercy. We also released forgiveness to the UEFA and other officials who had insisted that the match was played in an unfit stadium. We blessed Brussels, Heysel, Belgium and Italy and read various scriptures. We called on the Lord to bring reconciliation and healing with no idea of what God would do or how He would do it.

On the way out of the stadium television presenters, who were preparing to commentate on the match, stopped us. They asked us if we had come to watch the match and we explained to them why we had come, and the next thing we knew our apology was being broadcast across Belgium television!

MONS

If you have read my previous book "Extravagant Fire" you may recall that I spent over eight years serving my Local Authority on the Sefton Local Strategic Partnership. This was a strategic group of Directors and Chief

Executives from the Police, Health, Fire, Local Authority, Colleges, business and many more who met to determine the future plans for the Borough of Sefton. I was appointed to represent the residents and I knew Graham Haywood who was the Chief Executive Officer for Sefton Metropolitan Borough Council. Sefton is twinned with Mons in Belgium and in 2004, Sefton and Mons happened to be celebrating the fortieth anniversary of their twinning. I had a little chat with Graham who gave us lots of information and arranged for us to be given an official welcome and tour of Mons.

Mons is the capital of Bergen and was established at the top of a hill, around a 7th century monastery founded by St. Waudru. It has a population of 91,000 people and the Flemish name, Bergen means "mountains". Mons is a place full of huge superstitions and traditions. The area was founded on coal mining and the subsequent closure of most of the mines had caused economic hardship. Interestingly, for the British, Mons was the scene of their first battle in the First World War and their last at the end of the war.

We arrived in Mons on an extremely cold and very, very wet day! On arrival Patrick (our tour guide from Mons) took us around the ancient Town Hall and Collegiate Church. The front door of the Town Hall was actually a door within a door, within a door. The Door-keeper would choose which of the doors would be opened depending upon the time of the day and who was coming in. The largest door would be opened if a horse and rider were coming in. The middle door would be opened for someone on foot. The smallest door would be used at night and would mean that anyone entering had to stoop quite low to get through. In the past, if they were regarded as an enemy they would have their head cut off as they came through the door. Women were then brought in to remove the dead bodies and wash away the blood!

So we entered the Town Hall with great caution making sure there was nobody waiting with a sword! Patrick then led us into some of the major rooms of power and authority. Patrick was carrying the keys to the Town

Hall, which were 10 inches long and the biggest set of keys we had ever seen. The Lord told me to pray over the huge keys and I wondered how on earth I would do that as Patrick was so proud of his keys and was holding on to them very tightly.

Suddenly a thought flashed through my mind – "Patrick" I asked, "Could you take a photo of us holding your set of keys, as we have never seen such a big set of keys before?" Patrick was very willing and Norma, Jean and I (who all lived in Sefton) took hold of the keys whilst the others gathered around and Patrick took our photo. As the keys were in our hands we quietly prayed over them and commanded that every unrighteous thing that had been connected to Sefton would be locked up to release Sefton from any bad influences through the twinning.

We gave Patrick the keys back and we continued the tour. Patrick was about to take us into one of the main function rooms when the ancient locks would not open, despite Patrick's best efforts with the keys. Poor Patrick could not understand why the doors would not unlock. This had never happened before, but we knew it was a sign from the Lord that He had answered our prayers.

We were then led to the Collegiate Church that was founded by St Waudru, a married woman and mother of four healthy grown up children. As a couple they decided to separate and her husband, Count of Hainault joined a monastery. St Waudru determined to join a convent, however as she was not a virgin (the essential requirement for women) she was therefore rejected. Not put off too easily in 656AD she started her own. She stood on the hill in Mons and declared that everything she could see belonged to her - talk about claiming the ground! The whole area was a major coalfield that was later exploited to the full.

We realised now why the Lord had led us - eight women and a piece of coal to stand in the gap and to repent for the manipulation and control of

St Waudru and her canonesses. St Waudru quickly attracted young women whose families paid for them to stay at the Collegiate, whilst they looked for eligible bachelors for them to marry. Anyone who moved to the area had to pay substantial rent to St Waudru and she rapidly gathered huge wealth.

St Waudru and the ladies became known as the Canonesses and they ruled and reigned the region through manipulation and control. Families, afraid that their children born dead in childbirth would go to hell, without being baptised, would bring them to the altar within the Collegiate Church where St Waudru was said to perform miracles. We were told that the altar stone was so cold that the babies' bodies would jerk, causing their parents to believe the baby would live long enough to be baptized before dying.

The relics of St Waudru are still kept in the Collegiate Church. They cut off her head and stored that in one part of the Collegiate and the rest of the body is stored over the altar to this day. Each May the relics are placed upon a carriage and driven around the whole of Mons to bring "good luck" to the city.

The carriage was stored in the Church and in the area behind the carriage, was a huge clock with the fingers broken and the numbers missing. Alongside it was a distorted skeleton representing the grim reaper and the image of death. At the front of the carriage was the Masons' chapel. Once again we declared that Sefton would be cut off from all unrighteousness that was manifesting in Mons. A very strange church!

We had an opportunity to pray for our guide, Patrick who seemed deeply touched by the reality of God's love instead of the religion and superstition to which he was accustomed. As we left, Patrick recommended we visit the Mundaneum.

Over lunch we had another opportunity to pray, before we went back out into the cold rain to the Mundaneum. This was a very strange place with a huge globe rotating upon its axis under a ceiling, painted to look like a star-filled sky. It all looked very beautiful and a great reminder of the awesomeness of God and His creative perfection. Bizarrely all around the walls of the three-floored building were row upon row of drawers filled with index cards. Apparently, before computers were invented, two men had determined to collect and store all the information in the world. The drawers were covered with voile sheets upon which hung very strange and disturbing images. For example, there was an image of a bath full of blood and the words Palestine/Israel. Many of the images were clearly anti-Israel, anti-Bush and anti-Blair. Again we took some time here to stop and pray.

After a very weird and wet day, we made our way back to our hosts' home and were thrilled to be invited to spend the evening with the worship group from Vineyard. We had a wonderful time of praise, worship and fellowship. The Holy Spirit blessed us with His presence as we worshipped Him together.

WATERLOO

We made the first of our many visits to the European Parliament where there was still a great deal of construction work going on in those days. Outside the building there is a disgusting statue of Europa, holding the Euro aloft, out of the reach of the men who are worshipping her from below. Again we prayed here and called for God's intervention.

We then travelled to Waterloo, the very poignant site of the famous battle where the Duke of Wellington led his troops to a great victory. We visited the Panoramic Exhibition, which displayed the scene and the sounds of the battlefield, as it would actually have been. This was very moving as we saw Wellington upon his horse striding through the dead bodies of men and horses to bring victory over Napoleon. The scripture from Psalm 91:7 came to mind: *"a thousand may fall at your side, ten thousand at your right hand, but it will not come near you."*

Five of us ascended the mound - all 356 steps! It was bitterly cold but beautifully clear and we could see for many miles. We stopped at the top for some time to pray, spiritually cutting Waterloo (a place near to Liverpool, named after the battle) off from the death and destruction of this painful place. Interestingly, just as we finished praying, four Americans arrived, who just so happened to have come from Washington DC - the next place for our coal delivery.

In the following years we visited the battlefield of Waterloo several times. During one of those times the Lord spoke to us:

> *"This is the place where the battle for Europe was turned and there is an anointing here to be picked up, for those who will stand to see Europe turned back to God."*

There are many stories about the battle of Waterloo, but one story we found fascinating was about the actual day of the battle. Apparently, the fields were dreadfully wet and it was going to be impossible to move the canons into position. Just before the battle was about to start the little Catholic Church across the field rang the bells for Mass and many of Napoleon's men dropped their weapons and went to Church.

The church service delayed the start of the battle, giving Field Marshal Blucher and the Prussian army time to come to the aid of the Duke of Wellington and his men. Could it have been that the outcome of the whole battle and the future of Europe were turned all because of a church service?

BRUSSELS VINEYARD CHURCH

On the Sunday morning I spoke at the Vineyard Church service located in their old building and just happened to be the day when they would be relocating to their new building. I began by explaining our journey and apologising once again for the dreadful behaviour of some of the Liverpool fans. We did not know it at the time, but there were two families there who had lost members of their family at the Heysel Stadium. God moved very powerfully as they received our apology, and there was a good response as people came for prayer at the end of the meeting.

Later that Sunday evening we gathered together again, but this time in the new church building. Many people turned out despite the very cold temperatures, to seek God's face for the future of the Church in the new building. We left them the piece of coal with one of our fire flags. We had the opportunity to pray and prophecy over them that the Lord was going to send His fire and that they would see a multiplication of their congregation. Within the first year in the new building the church doubled in size! Keith, the Pastor, and Mike then led a time of prayer for our team. A word was given that we would be travelling to many nations of the world.

Time for reconciliation and healing

Three and a half months after our trip to the Heysel Stadium, Liverpool drew Juventus in the Champions League. As it was announced I struggled for my breath and wept like a baby! I knew this was the Lord, giving Liverpool an opportunity to demonstrate their sorrow and extend the hand of friendship.

In April 2005, Liverpool FC and Juventus met to play in the Champions League quarter-final. This was the first time they had played each other since the Heysel disaster almost twenty years ago. The Liverpool Echo newspaper headlines carried the words we had prayed in November, "Heysel healing and reconciliation".

We visited Anfield Stadium the day the tickets were issued for the Juventus and Liverpool FC match, and asked if they would allow us in to pray. The man on the gate looked a little surprised and unsure but went off to ask his boss. This process was repeated several times until most of the staff of Anfield knew we were coming in to pray. For the benefit of those who support Liverpool – no we did not touch the turf! We went in to pray and asked the Lord for a real spirit of repentance to be poured out. We prayed that Liverpool would be the friendliest place on earth for all the Italian fans that visited from Juventus.

This first meeting of Liverpool FC and Juventus since that tragic night in Brussels twenty years earlier was sure to be an emotive one for all concerned. However with great humility, Liverpool FC honoured the memory of the thirty-nine victims of the Heysel disaster. There was a number of commemorative gestures leading up to the Champions League tie with Juventus:

- A friendly match between Liverpool and Juventus fans at the Liverpool FC Academy.
- The Liverpool Kop displayed a mosaic as every supporter held a card aloft. Together the mosaic featured the word "Amicizia", Italian for "friendship", alongside a Liver Bird (the Liverpool crest) and the respective club colours were displayed. At the same time they also held a one-minute silence prior to the kick-off.
- Every visiting fan received a free four-page brochure in Italian aimed at promoting friendship and understanding between the supporters. The front cover carried the club crests and words of welcome. On the back were the words: "We Are Sorry. You'll Never Walk Alone."
- Each visiting fan also received a special wristband in red, white and black with the inscription "friendship" written in both Italian and English.
- The Liverpool Echo newspaper headlines also displayed "We are so sorry" with the names of all those who died at the Heysel stadium.

Everything was done here in Liverpool to apologise and put things right, although sadly that would never bring back the lives lost. As we prayed, the people of Liverpool humbled themselves and apologised. We knew that God was blessing our region, as Liverpool went through to the final.

If you were a gambling person you would say the odds were stacked against Liverpool for the match against Chelsea - but then most people had not perceived that the favour of God was upon Liverpool FC to bring them victory.

After the semi-final with Chelsea, this was a headline from the Liverpool FC's official web site "Just five months ago Liverpool, were four minutes away from being knocked out of the Champions League". Further down the same article is this paragraph referring to the semi-final victory: "But this was not supposed to happen, was it? This is the same Liverpool team which has this season been described as the worst in 40 years".

Within the CWM team we were very confident that the Lord's hand was upon this from the very beginning, when we set foot in the Heysel Stadium, to Liverpool FC arriving in Istanbul to play A.C.Milan in the European Cup many months later. Liverpool played very hard each match leading up to the Champion's League Cup Final on 25th May 2005 in Istanbul. At half time Liverpool were 3-0 down and the odds of them winning were 350/1. You can understand as we later reflected on an amazing victory, why we acknowledged the hand of God.

It was as though Liverpool FC were taken to the point where it had to be God for them to win! Liverpool FC received the crown as the champions of Europe 2005. Across Liverpool and the nation the celebrations were euphoric. Television and newspaper reporters spoke of the "Miracles of Istanbul". On 26th May 2005, the Daily Express declared Liverpool's European Cup Victory as a miracle and headlines were full of biblical quotes.

Is God interested in football? Who would know? However, we know that God loves his people and He loves the land. His word in 2 Chronicles 7:14 says *"If My people who are called by My name, will humble themselves and pray and seek My face and turn from their wicked ways, then I will hear from heaven and will forgive their sin and will heal their land".*

We believe this is about God wanting to bring healing and reconciliation between people, football clubs, between cities, between nations and as a result we have seen the start of that reconciliation and healing.

Glory to God! What an awesome answer to our prayers as we saw a real financial blessing come to our region as a result of this, with a renewed hope and expectation released. I believe that the Lord is pouring out His favour. We are seeing such an amazing turn around in this region as Christians are putting their faith in God to turn around impossible situations.

I am reminded of the image of the Liverpool FC's open top bus touring the streets, which were crowded with almost a million people. The front of the bus had a huge banner with LIVERPOOL and images of the five European silver cups. Five is the number of grace and when you have won the European Cup five times you are allowed to keep the cup.

Dutch Sheets sent us a word of encouragement shortly before this.

> "We had experienced plenty of opportunities to be disappointed in the past but that we would not be disappointed this time".

I am sure Dutch Sheets was not talking about the football, but about what is happening across the region, as we are starting to see a supernatural and physical transformation.

WASHINGTON DC

By July 2006 we were waiting for the right opportunity to deliver the fourth piece of coal to Washington DC. Several opportunities had come but we needed the right one. It is so important that we do not just go because we see an attractive opportunity - we need to go when the Lord calls us to. It is only when we go in God's timing that we connect with the divine appointments that the Lord has prepared for us.

An American friend of ours, Martha Lucia had been living in the UK for five years and was returning to live in the USA. Martha has a beautiful home in Florida and had kindly invited me to go to stay with her, but I declined, as God had not told me to go. I explained to Martha that the Lord had only told me to go to Washington DC in order to deliver our fourth piece of coal. It sounds strange but Martha totally understood and instead she invited us to go with her to Washington DC in July 2006. We were invited to go to represent the British and to pray in various strategic buildings in Washington DC, including the White House! This sounded like a God opportunity to me.

As we were planning the trip a division arose in the team, and one person who was going to come caused some difficulties. I made the decision to stop the trip, as I did not want the team to be in disunity. Unity is one of our most powerful gifts and we do try to protect it. However, over the next three weeks I became very depressed and I eventually asked God, "What is wrong with me Lord?" The Lord responded immediately and said, "I never told you to cancel the trip to Washington DC!"

Oh my goodness, I learned a very important lesson that day. I had presumed that because we were in disunity it would be wrong for any of the team to go. I had made a big decision without even consulting God. I repented straight away and declared that if God wanted me to go I would go, even if it meant I would be going on my own. When I told the others what God had said, the person causing the difficulties was very offended and eventually left the team. However, God was not offended, in fact He was really pleased. He released such favour and anointing upon the rest of the team that we were totally amazed at what He had planned for us. How close we were to missing what God had in store for us.

As we were preparing to fly out to Washington DC we were aware that there had been fifteen murders in fifteen days, in the very community we were going to be staying in. We prayed and released peace and an end to the violent deaths. We also bought a figurine called the "blessing of peace" which the Lord told us we would need to give to someone as a gift.

The American contingent of the team, were staying in the best hotels but as Graham and Sue Derrig, Ian Yates and I had paid for our flights, we could not afford the price of the hotels too. Martha arranged for us to stay with some wonderful local Christians who lived in Washington DC. I got to stay in an apartment with four lovely ladies and Ian stayed in the apartment below.

One of those ladies was Liza Heavener who worked for one of the Senators in the Capitol Building. Liza arranged a tour of the building for us. Awesome! We visited places behind the scenes where regular tours do not take you, plus we got to meet people and pray in some very strategic places. We were thrilled to be in the Senate Chamber as they debated legislation to change and improve the voting rights of Americans. It was said by Senators that it was a very important and significant time for America. It was amazing to know we were actually there at that moment in history, praying and watching! For me there are no words to really describe this incredible experience! It really felt like an out of body experience as we pinched ourselves in disbelief.

Liza was very knowledgeable, pointing out each Senator, those who were Christians and those who were the candidates likely to run for President next time around. Senator Hillary Clinton (representing New York) and Senator Barack Obama (representing Illinois) were pointed out to us. Liza told us that many people believed that Barack Obama would either be the next Martin Luther King, the next President or he would be assassinated! Liza told us that he is an awesome man of God who cannot be bought, who is prepared to speak the truth and when he speaks, people stop and listen!

God told us Senator Barack Obama would be the future President of the United States and to pray for him. It was amazing to consider that we were literally inches away from the future first African American President of the United States. We never let go of the word that God planned for him to be President, despite the discouragement we received from our American friends. We took that word from God seriously and prayed for him many times over the coming years and continue to do so.

We actually saw Congressman John Lewis enter the Senate Chamber. John is a wonderful and very powerful Christian who famously stood shoulder to shoulder with Martin Luther King, the most significant American civil rights leader. Martin Luther King said *"The ultimate measure of a man is not where he stands in moments of comfort and convenience, but where he stands at times of challenge and controversy. The true neighbour will risk his position, his prestige and even his life for the welfare of others."*

John had been battered to the point of death as he crossed a bridge with civil rights marchers. He quite rightly held great esteem and honour in the Senate and we were overwhelmed to have seen him.

There was a sense of awe in the Chamber, as Senator Ted Kennedy rose to his feet to speak and ask for unanimous consent on the legislation. Later we watched as ninety-eight out of the hundred Senators cast their votes. The vote was exactly ninety-eight consenting so they got unanimous consent, as two were absent.

This is the text from the newspaper headlines written by Carl Heusen and published 21st July 2006.

Unanimous consent Vote of 98-0
Senate approves 25 Year extension of Voting Rights Act

Washington, July 20. The Senate voted overwhelmingly on Thursday to extend the landmark Voting Rights Act for another 25 years, as lawmakers of both parties said federal supervision was still required to protect the ability of minorities and the disadvantaged to cast ballots in some regions of the country.

"Despite the progress these states have made in upholding the right to vote, it is clear the problems still exist," said Senator Barack Obama, Democrat of Illinois.

We were amazed that we had visited the Capitol Building just as the Voting Rights legislation was passing through the Senate Chamber. The very legislation that made it possible for Barack Obama to become the first African American President, and the forty-fourth President of the United States, on 20th January 2009, just thirty months later.

Later that same day we went into the White House, as you do! We had provided our security information for screening over two months prior to our arrival in order to get permission to go in. The Lord spoke to me and told me to take a small bag in with me, containing some scriptures, my glasses and the piece of coal. That sounds a simple thing to do but when you are told that no bags could be taken in, it becomes more of a challenge. We had to leave our bags with a lady outside who would look after them for us.

As we queued to go into the White House, others in the team noticed my little bag and told me to leave it with the lady appointed to look after them. I did not know what God was going to ask me to do, but I knew He wanted me to take this little bag into the White House. So despite several requests, I stubbornly kept hold of the bag and as I drew near to the security screens I wondered what would happen.

The security was just like airport security - very thorough. As I got to the front of the queue, my heart was thumping, as the Security Officer walked around the security scanner and came to me. He took the bag from me and simply walked back to his post. As I walked through he put the bag back into my hands and not a word was spoken. I wonder if he was an angel?

We walked around the White House in awe, wondering what difference our visit would make and why the Lord had opened these prestigious doors to us. There was so much to see and even more to perceive, as I was listening carefully to hear what was on God's heart. We were clearly being watched, as we walked from room to room, and by now my heart was thumping so loud I was not sure I would hear what God wanted me to do when He spoke.

It was a beautiful building full of history and with such a sense of holding the future destinies of people and nations. Meanwhile, we were told that President George Bush was in the house watching a movie! It was wonderful to be able to pray there and to read the scriptures the Lord had laid on our hearts. However, there was still a sense that God had not finished there.

As we were led out of the front door of the White House, the Lord spoke to me. Oh my word! I knew that the FBI and goodness knows who else would be watching us all, as we left the home of the most powerful man in the world and now God decided to speak to me!

The Lord told me to plant the scriptures I had brought in my bag. I quickly and silently cried out to God "Where Lord?" Everything was happening so quickly and I could not see how I would be able to plant anything. Over the sound of my heart pounding in my ears, I heard the Lord tell me to stoop down to fix my shoe. As I stooped down, the Lord told me to plant the scriptures under the shrub just by the column near to the front door.

I have to admit I was anxious that I was being watched and could be in deep trouble. However, as I arose and life continued without any fuss, I wondered if the Lord had hidden me, as I was not challenged at all. I also wondered, why the Lord would want me to plant scriptures under a shrub at the front door of the White House. However, the Lord looks for our simple obedience even when it does not make sense to us.

You may be wondering what happened to the piece of coal? We went to Church with Liza where we were introduced to Pastor Dennis who is a member of the Apostolic Network of Washington DC. Pastor Dennis was very happy to receive the coal and the prophetic word that went with it, on behalf of the leaders and Apostles of Washington DC.

We felt it was right to present the "blessing of peace" figurine to Sandy Grady who was the Prayer Co-ordinator for Washington DC. She was amongst a number of people who were taken out through illness and was not able to participate in the prayer assignments after spending years praying and preparing for it. We were so disappointed that we were not going to meet her. However, guess who was sitting in the row in front of us in Church? At the end of the service we presented Sandy with "the blessing of peace" figurine, prayed for her and the city of Washington DC. She was deeply moved, as in the prayer meeting prior to the Church service she had prayed for peace to be deposited and left in DC.

One day after a tiring and very busy day, we had a funny yet miraculous moment in a car on our way back to our accommodation. We jumped into a taxi outside of Union Station, which as you can imagine is very busy with heavy traffic. The car drove forward a few metres and then all of a sudden the taxi driver was struggling to get the car to drive forward. The car shook and juddered but refused to go forward. The driver was very embarrassed as the car was now stopping the flow of peak traffic. People were honking their horns from every direction and our poor driver was getting very anxious. The driver was doing all he could to get the car moving and he did actually get it to move but it only went backwards!

We offered to get out and walk but the driver insisted he would get us to our destination safely. As suddenly as the problems with the car had started, they stopped, and the car drove smoothly the few blocks to our accommodation. However, as we arrived clearly something very wrong had happened.

Moments after the car problems had started there was a shooting right outside the home where we were staying. Had the car driven normally we would have arrived just as the shooting was happening. We were certain that there had been angelic intervention on our behalf to keep us safe. Thankfully nobody was seriously injured and during our visit to Washington DC there were actually no murders. A breakthrough indeed!

Our trips are often made special by the divine appointments God prepares for us. One of those divine appointments was made by Graham and Sue, who met Linda and her husband Jeff Herbert who Pastor a Church just outside Washington DC. Linda also happened to be a high-ranking officer in the army and worked in the Pentagon. Lieutenant Colonel Linda Herbert is an awesome woman of God already in high office within the Army but certainly destined for higher.

You are not allowed to take a photograph outside of the Pentagon because the security is so tight and we had not completed any security checks. However, Linda kindly offered to take us in to pray and we found ourselves walking through the corridors of the most secure place in the world. It is a vast place and despite over seventeen miles of corridors, it takes only seven minutes to walk between any two points in the building. There are five rings, five floors, five sides, five corners and five acres in the centre courtyard.

Linda worked in the very area of the Pentagon that five years earlier, was hit by an American Airlines Boeing 757 airliner as it crashed into the Pentagon at 9.38am. Linda took us to the scene of the crash where on 11th September 2001 their lives changed forever. Linda's story of that day and what happened is just simply miraculous but it is her story to tell and you can read it in her book "The Pentagon Miracle: An Eyewitness Account".[1]

Linda showed us the photographs and the map of where everyone was seated and located at the time of the impact. We saw the photographs of her twenty four colleagues (from her section) who had died and she told us of the funeral she had personally conducted. It was very moving and we were all very close to tears.

It was amazing to see that within one year of the plane hitting the building, it was completely rebuilt and on 9th September 2002 rededicated. We were later taken to see the memorial and the Chapel. We prayed that the Lord would continue to bring healing to the survivors and their families from the injuries, trauma and the shock. It was good to see the Chapel full as a communion service was being conducted. Deborah told us that there are many Christians working at the Pentagon and her husband is one of the Chaplain's there. We were given an army version of the Gideon New Testament.

We were able to go right into the Media Room where Donald Rumsfeld and others make all the press announcements and broadcasts. It was overwhelming to be there, where all of the global media microphones assemble to hear the latest news from the Pentagon. As we stood on the plinth, we looked out over the seats reserved for CNN, ABC, Fox News, BBC, Sky News and many more. We took the opportunity to declare the Lordship of Jesus over the media and the nations from the official place where declarations are released out across the world.

It was just as we finished doing this, that a guy came in to see what we were up to. He had probably come in to throw us out, but we simply said we had come from Liverpool, England to pray for them and to pray for their government, like this was the most normal thing in the world. As soon as he heard our accents he was lovely and commented that we came from the same place as the Beatles. "Yes", I replied, "actually our office is in Strawberry Fields. Would you like to take our photograph?" He took some photographs for us and then we spent a couple of minutes praying for him. We thanked God for saving Linda's life and for the work and ministry of God's people within the Pentagon.

Later in the afternoon, we visited Arlington Cemetery, which is a really high place. We were able to look over DC from the hill where J F Kennedy is buried, with his wife and brother. It is a huge place and swamped with tourists. We felt so sorry for the soldiers on duty guarding the tomb of the "Unknown Soldier", as the temperature must have been 100 degrees. We could understand from watching the soldiers' ceremony why the Americans love our changing of the guards at Buckingham Palace so much.

We popped into the International HQ of the World Bank. The security was very tight but the door was wide open, so we just simply walked in. We asked if we could pray in the reception area and they were pleased for us to pray. Their strap line is, "Our dream is a world free of poverty", so we prayed in agreement with that and declared that the accounts that were withholding money from the poor would be opened.

We then pottered over to the International Monetary Fund (IMF) HQ a couple of blocks away and asked them if we could come in to pray. The security guards were fun. They said we could not go in, but once they heard we were from Liverpool they were happy to very quietly suggest we go into the IMF book shop just a few yards away and that would actually take us right into the building! Once again the security was very tight and you needed to have ID, which Graham and Sue had not brought with them. We quietly prayed and then the doors opened for us and in we went! We called for the wealth of the nations to be released and distributed fairly to those it had been stolen from in the past, e.g. Africa.

We later visited the Abraham Lincoln Monument, which was certainly something not to be missed whilst we were there. It felt like a very powerful place spiritually, as we stood where Martin Luther King had stood on 28th August 1963 to make his famous "I have a dream" speech in front of 250,000 people.

Abraham Lincoln not only saved the Union, preserving both its government and boundaries, he reinvigorated the nation's founding principal - that all men are created equal. Carved into the Memorial there are amazing quotes from speeches made by Abraham Lincoln which included the information that an eighth of the population of America were African slaves! We had never dreamt it was such a high number.

This is one of the texts I found so inspiring:

"Both read the same Bible, and pray to the same God; and each invokes His aid against the other. It may seem strange that any men should dare to ask a just God's assistance in wringing their bread from the sweat of other men's faces; but let us judge not that we be not judged. The prayers of both could not be answered; that of neither has been answered fully. The Almighty has his own purposes. Woe unto the world because of offences! For it must needs be that offences come; but woe to that man by whom the offence cometh!"

We left Washington DC totally amazed as we reviewed all of the incredible doors the Lord had opened for us.

---

[1] available at http://www.pentagonmiracle.com or from

http://www.amazon.co.uk/The-Pentagon-Miracle-Eyewitness-Account/dp/0972318518

BERLIN

Every step along our journey has been important and prepared the way for what comes next. Our journey to Berlin was one of those steps that became very significant in the days ahead.

In 1884 twelve European nations, the USA and Russia met to greedily and arrogantly, "cut up Africa like a cake" without the consent of the nations themselves. Many of the nations were used and abused in some of the most horrific ways. Several Christian leaders came together with a heart to do something about this and to seek God for healing these nations.

The process of reconciliation started six years earlier and involved, "uncovering the sins" that resulted from that 1884 Conference. Along with others from across Europe we were invited to go to Berlin in 2005 for the European and African Reconciliation Conference. We were invited to represent Liverpool because of Liverpool's historic involvement in the Transatlantic Slave Trade.

Berlin was a real challenge in so many ways and yet in the midst of the pain of the spiritual journey, we really had some laughs. We struggled with the language barriers, as we did not speak any German and most of the people we encountered did not speak English. We ended up with some very interesting meals, as we had not ordered what we thought we had!

We arrived at the conference and there were people there, representing all of the European and African nations. We had a powerful time of worship and then we had to go into groups according to the nations we were representing. It was then up to each group to determine which things they were willing to apologise for. The following day the room was reorganised with a large table in the centre. It certainly felt like a very somber moment, as we all gathered around with the Europeans on one side of the table and the Africans on the other.

The representatives from each European nation stood to their feet in turn, standing opposite the representatives from the African nations that had been colonised by that particular European nation. Two prayer ministry leaders from the UK, Brian Mills and Chris Seaton stood on behalf of the UK to repent for the terrible things the UK had committed against Ghana, Sierra Leone, Gambia, Nigeria, South Africa, Sudan, Uganda, and other nations.

There was a time of deep repentance and sorrow with tears flowing from those making the apologies and those receiving them. Our African friends were quick to release forgiveness and to look to God to bring the breakthroughs for their nations. These wounds run deep and it was time for them to be cleansed so that healing could start to come.

One sight that will remain with me is of two precious women. One was a German lady and the other was from one of the African nations previously colonised by Germany. These two ladies were entwined, arms wrapped around one another and sobbing, as they looked to God to bring healing and reconciliation to both of their nations.

The November gathering culminated in a statement drawn up by ministry leaders Roger Mitchell (Passion UK), Chris Seaton (Peaceworks) and Brian Mills (Interprayer):

"It is our prayer that this will lead to many continuing acts of love and restitution from our nation towards those nations sinned against. We recognise that this is not the whole story. The Africans were gracious to remind us of the legacy of the Gospel that was brought by European missionaries, and of the contribution made to their well-being through education, medicine and certain infrastructures.

We were so grateful to God for bringing us to the conclusion of this Reconciliation Process in Berlin. It was a very moving occasion, where we were part of a group of representatives from around 20 European and 25 African nations present, committed to prayer and reconciliation. The focus of the event was a "solemn assembly" where we re-enacted the posture of the conference in 1884-1885 that concentrated on carving up of Africa by Europe. Delegates from 14 European nations were at the table - but in contrast to 1885, we had African delegates there too. There were declarations of confession, repentance and forgiveness. In all it was a beginning for a new start for Africa & Europe we believe."

The repentance and forgiveness was deep and powerful, and yet I was disturbed. It bothered me that our mighty God, who knows all things, could have stopped this horrendous manipulation and control of a whole continent, but did not. Why was that? Father God will always turn what Satan meant for our harm and bring something good out of it – therefore my question was – what did God want to bring out of this process besides the repentance and forgiveness? As I continued to seek the Lord I believe the Lord gave me some revelation and I include the word below.

AFRICA & EUROPEAN RECONCILIATION CONFERENCE

"To our brothers and sisters from the nations of Africa, God has not called you here as an aggregation of African nations but as a congregation.

A continent of beautiful and passionate people brought together with a common fundamental purpose as in Acts 2:1-8.

The Lord has drawn you together to wash you, to heal you and to restore you, in order for you to take hold of your identity and destiny (Joshua 18:3).

For God created you to be a people and a land of vast riches and abundant fruitfulness.

The enemy knew God's plans and came to steal, kill and destroy. But that which was intended to harm you, God will use for good to accomplish His plans and the saving of many lives (Genesis 50:20).

For God has been teaching you so very much through your brokenness. You have learned humility and have laid down your lives. This is a requirement of true disciples – a people that God has been searching for.

For God is looking for those that He can pour His Spirit into, to speak to the nations. You have been taught the languages of the nations and through your brokenness He is giving you a voice that the nations are ready to receive and listen to.

First God is saying to you that you must take back your spiritual heritage, which was stolen from you (1 Sam 30:18).

You must rise up as the awesome people God has created you to be. Africa is like the womb and God is preparing to birth new life across the nations. It is time for the umbilical cord to be cut. It is time for your release. It is time for you to rise up and to release the sound of the worshipping warriors, the sound that will bring healing to the nations.

God opened Africa in order to further the kingdom of God and He has given you the voice and humility to do that."

This word was quickly typed up and photocopied to ensure that everyone from Africa could be given a copy to take back with them. I believe that it actually went into every African nation. I saw an image of a global prayer day with fires going out from Africa around the world.

We were only there for a few days but we found time to visit The Reichstag Building, the home of the German Parliament. We walked up into the dome of the building which gives great views, both into the Parliamentary chamber and out over the city of Berlin. We heard that an Architect from Liverpool had designed that part of the building. What a great place to pray!

As we came out, it was going dark and we looked up at the Brandenburg Gate just a few yards away. It looked beautiful all lit up and we were reminded that since the Berlin Wall had come down, it now symbolises German unity. We walked across and stood in the gate in awe of the freedom that had come with such a high price.

Opposite the gate was a small remnant of the Berlin Wall that had stood from 13th August 1961 to 9th November 1989. The wall had divided East from West, separating families and loved ones. It was almost impenetrable and people had lost their lives attempting to scale it. However, people all over the world had been praying for many years and eventually it was demolished. We were given a couple of pieces of the wall which we brought home with us, to remind us that even the biggest walls can come down.

UGANDA

Our journey into Africa began when God spoke to us in July 2005. Bob Geldof was leading the "Make Poverty History" campaign and challenging the G8 leaders to keep their promises to help to eradicate the debts of the African nations. The Lord spoke to us and said, *"He had forgiven Liverpool for the sin of the Slave Trade and that He was now releasing the blessing, but we needed to sow life into Africa".*

We asked the Lord, "How do you want us to do that?" God spoke to us clearly and we were given a vision to partner with Arnold Muwonge, to help develop the Kampala Children's Centre in Uganda. Arnold's vision was to build one hundred houses that will be home for twelve children each. We knew God was challenging us to raise enough money to build a home, to be called Abundant House. This house would be a prophetic love gift from Liverpool to Africa, declaring a release of the abundance of God into the lives of the children.

So we set about raising the £14,000 we needed. It started slowly, but people began to catch the vision and before we knew it people were cycling the Leeds to Liverpool canal, completing sponsored silences, selling clothes on eBay, running races and with amazing generosity we raised £21,000!

Abundant House was built and the invitation went out to see who would come to Uganda as part of the team. Graham and Sue Derrig, Doreen Kelly, Hazel Dykins, Liz Boote, Angela Roberts and Anita Gowan all responded. Graham kindly offered to organise the trip and the date was set for 6th January 2007.

The flights went well from Manchester to Entebbe. We landed in the middle of the night to the sound of crickets and an anticipation of what God was going to do. People had been so generous and we were loaded down with aid including a sewing machine, clothing and even a space hopper! We had been advised by people who had been to Uganda before, to leave our best clothes at home and to dress very simply, so that is what we prepared for.

We arrived in Uganda late on Saturday night to a warm welcome and we were driven to our Guest House in Ntinda on the outskirts of Kampala. Meanwhile Graham and Sue went on a medical mission for a few days.

The next morning, we awoke refreshed, but with no idea of what to expect. We had dressed very simply as we had been advised. The temperature was already very hot and sticky as we ate our breakfast. Our friend Arnold arrived with instructions for us all. He turned to Hazel, Liz and Angela and said, "You will all be coming to KCC Church with me and meeting the children for the first time." They were of course thrilled. "What about us?" I quickly asked. He looked at us, smiled and said, "Oh, Sue you are going to speak in Pastor John's Church and you can take Anita and Doreen with you". "What? Are you joking?" Of course Arnold was not joking and he told us that Pastor John would be along in a few minutes to collect us.

So with absolutely no preparation whatsoever we were collected by Pastor John to minister in his Church. Pastor John had a smile that could light up the world, as he encouraged us to step into his car. He was very proud of his car, as most Ugandans do not even possess a bicycle, let alone a car. However, the car was a sight to behold, but certainly not to travel in!

Pastor John's pride and joy was covered in thick red dust inside and out, with a very badly cracked front window screen that could implode at any moment, except for the tape holding it together. The seats were all torn with the stuffing missing and covered over by loose scatter cushions. Most of the windows would not open at all as they were stuck fast, whilst only a couple of the seat belts were operating. So completely putting our trust in God, we climbed into Pastor John's car and chatted away to disguise our fear. We drove for about fifteen minutes through the busiest and worst streets we had ever experienced in our lives. Most of the roads were simply muddy dirt tracks with the biggest humps and potholes you can possibly imagine.

Here we were, three ladies who had never been to Africa before, being led off with a man we had only met seconds before, in a car that should have been condemned long ago, to a place we did not know, to do something we had not prepared for! Welcome to Uganda!

The Church was like most Ugandan Churches with a dirt floor, corrugated metal roof and wooden walls. It had several tiers and simple wooden benches for most of the congregation to sit on. We were invited to sit on white plastic garden chairs that were reserved for the special guests. The people were truly beautiful, greeting us with great excitement and were dressed like they were going to a wedding. So much for us being told to dress simply, we now felt embarrassed, shabby and underdressed.

Actually Pastor John was really wonderful and he was thrilled to welcome us to his Church. The meeting started with beautiful African worship which, even though we did not understand the words, we adored. The men particularly touched our hearts as they worshipped and danced with such passion and joy.

Pastor John introduced Anita first. Anita gave a fabulous word to the Church and a challenging prophetic word to Pastor John. Doreen was next, part way through the power failed - very common in Uganda. Despite this Doreen was fabulous and remained unflustered whilst delivering a fantastic word.

Finally Pastor John introduced "Pastor Shue" and we all looked around expecting someone else to step up to the microphone. Everyone was clapping loudly with great anticipation but nobody stepped up. Once again Pastor John invited "Pastor Shue" to come to the microphone and nobody came. "Oh dear", I thought, "that is not good". Suddenly it dawned on me that they could not pronounce my name and "Pastor Shue" was actually me!

I had acquired an "H" just like Abram and Sara in Genesis 17:3 when Abram fell facedown, and God said to him, *"As for me, this is my covenant with you: You will be the father of many nations. No longer will you be called Abram; your name will be Abraham, for I have made you a father of many nations. I will make you very fruitful".*

In Genesis 17:15 God also said to Abraham *"As for Sarai your wife, you are no longer to call her Sarai; her name will be Sarah. I will bless her and will surely give you a son by her. I will bless her so that she will be the mother of nations; kings of peoples will come from her."*

God had made a clear covenant with Abraham and He promised him the land of Canaan, and that many descendants and nations would come from him. God highlighted this covenant promise in the name change from Abram to Abraham, as Abraham means '"father of many nations" and Sarah means "the mother of nations".

God was beginning our ministry in Africa and so complete with my new letter "H", Pastor Shue arose to speak from Philippians 3:10 and Isaiah 61. The word was very well received and at the end we were surprised when hundreds of people responded; I think people were coming from all the surrounding villages! Pastor John was delighted and took us home to meet his wife and family. Home was a humble cemented shack; the living room was cramped with a suite full of holes and some basic furniture. There were no ceilings to the rooms but a basic tin roof. His children came in one at a time and knelt at our feet to greet us. We were really honoured to spend some time praying for the family before we went back to our Guest House.

The rest of the team had a wonderful time at KCC Church and came back full of stories having seen Abundant House for the first time. The following day we all drove to KCC and I have to say that words simply cannot express the depths of poverty we saw as we travelled through the streets. However we also felt the deepest joy as we arrived at Destiny Avenue. This took us up to KCC with our first view of Abundant House and the other four homes. As we clambered off the minibus, the most amazing and beautiful children of KCC rushed around excitedly to welcome us. The whole experience was completely overwhelming. In fact I was virtually speechless!

When Arnold arrived in his car the children gathered around him obviously thrilled to see "Daddy". We were given a guided tour and introduced to the House Mothers. Arnold showed us around the Church and took us up to the hill where houses six and seven were about to be started. We were then led into Abundant House and it was really beautiful. Arnold introduced us to two ladies from Rwanda who had been in Abundant House for one month praying for our children before they arrived.

We later visited the Money Exchangers and changed the money that we had brought. We received 332,000 shillings in exchange for £100, so with what we had brought we suddenly became millionaires! That felt good, as I had never been a millionaire before. We returned to our Guest House and our first experience of life without power, as they frequently have power cuts. So we were very grateful for our torches.

The next day we went on safari and we enjoyed the beauty of Uganda as the van hurtled along - mile after mile of very bumpy and extremely dusty roads. I had made the mistake of asking the Lord for "Elephant encounters" and as we approached the River Nile we watched a herd of wild elephants grazing near the water's edge. We were overwhelmed and when a group of hippos emerged, I was reminded of the dancing hippos from the TV advert.

We crossed the River Nile on a flat bed ferry, arriving at our hotel exhausted, filthy and too late to go for the scheduled evening safari. We showered and went down to the pool to have a welcome dip. We might have missed the evening safari, but God brought the elephants to us! On the edge of the pool was a little wall and we suddenly heard the trees at the other side rustling. The elephants came as close as they could come, five elephants including a youngster, just doing what elephants do - feeding and foraging.

The following day we rose excitedly, ready for our safari and were joined by Simon (our Tour Guide) plus a gun! It was not long before we were "oooing" and "aaahing" admiring the incredible beauty of Uganda. The elephants, giraffes, birds and water buffalo all came out to display God's creative glory. The water buffalo were walking away and about to disappear, much to Hazel's disappointment, when we shouted, "Stop in the name of Jesus!" Suddenly they all came to an immediate stop and turned 180 degrees to face us. It looked as though they were actually posing for us and we were reminded of the scripture, "all of creation is groaning for the manifestation of the sons of God".

When an angry bull elephant appeared in the middle of the track, we were encouraged as we remembered that God had given Adam dominion over all the animals; and He had given that same dominion to us. However this was not a happy elephant and he was determined that he was not moving off the track. He was kicking up the dust and his ears were out, and he was roaring.

He began to move rapidly towards us and Gerard, our driver, stopped the vehicle immediately. We kept very still whilst praying earnestly. Our driver began to put his foot down on the accelerator to cause the engine to roar loudly, but he did not move. The elephant began to run, charging towards us and we had no choice but to use our authority. "Back off in the name of Jesus!" The elephant backed off and moved around the side of the vehicle. He then charged towards us again, so we repeated, "Back off in the name of Jesus!" before he backed off again. The prayer was very fervent!

We could see Gerard's reflection in the mirror, as he sweetly smiled, as though to fill us with confidence that this had happened many times before and we were quite safe. Later we discovered that he had never experienced this before and that Simon was not allowed to use his gun against the elephant, only against poachers! The elephant, who was recognisable by the hole in its left ear, had recently crushed and trampled a man to death. We were so glad that the Lord was with us.

Early the next morning we started our journey back and whilst crossing on the ferry over the Nile, we were warmly greeted by some Ugandan Liverpool fans, who gave us a heart-warming rendition of "You'll never walk alone". We had not expected that in the middle of the Nile!

We then proceeded to Murchison Falls where we met Henry, our Guide. He told us that Sir Roderick Murchison was a British Horticulturalist during the colonial days and the Falls were named after him. In 1961 there were heavy rains that birthed a beautiful new waterfall next to Murchison that the Ugandans named Freedom. The waterfalls are not large, for example Murchison is only forty-three metres high and seven metres wide. However, they are extremely powerful as the volume of water flowing through the narrowest place on the Nile is a massive three hundred cubic meters per second. I wonder who measured that! The force of the water causes a misty spray and as the sun shines upon the mist, beautiful dancing rainbows appear and disappear. The land itself sparkles and shines as though it is encrusted with precious stones. It is certainly a very beautiful place.

Suddenly the Spirit of God fell upon us and we began to really pray and cry out for the nation of Uganda. God told us to pray for the uprooting of the foundations of Kony and the Lord's Resistance Army (LRA) in order to release real freedom into the North of Uganda. As we prayed we clearly saw a dove rising up from the waters - a sign of the Holy Spirit and we knew something was shifting.

Upon our return to the Guest House we were immersed into darkness as the power supply had gone down again. I am sure the scene of me sitting inside my mosquito net with a miners' style torch on my head, trying to finish my preparations to speak at a conference the next day was very funny!

The Rising Tide Conference began with hundreds of extremely poor Pastors arriving after travelling for days, many without public transport or their own vehicles. They camped in the field with their wives and children.

The main speakers were Arnold Muwonge, Lee Martin and I. Lee is a wonderful and animated preacher who spends his time jumping on tables and chairs as he preaches. I was feeling slightly intimidated and quickly told Arnold that I would not be jumping on any tables! Arnold was full of passion and fire, preaching the most awesome teaching we have ever heard on leadership. It was a great pity that it was not recorded as I can think of many leadership teams who would benefit from hearing all that was brought. I was inspired by the whole atmosphere as the Leaders were spoken to in such an uncompromising way, without them taking offence and there was a great time of repentance.

We could not help but notice that the women were very, very broken and many had death all over them. They would not look you in the eye and would hang their heads heavily. The message of God's love for them was so significant and our team spent lots of time ministering to them.

On the final day of the conference there was a great sense of anticipation. Arnold introduced me by prophesying over me and it was very difficult to stand up after that! I spoke about Hannah and how she had to push through the difficulties and discouragements to birth the new move of God for her nation. I encouraged people to arise as Hannah did and to push through. I shared the prophetic words the Lord had given me in Berlin in November 2004 for the continent of Africa. I was amazed at how everything all fitted together so well and we then went into a time of intercession for Northern Uganda.

I shared what happened when we were at Murchison a few days earlier and how we believed it was a new day for Uganda. Arnold helped us to identify twenty of the most senior Pastors from the North of Uganda who were brought out to the front. They began to sing in their very powerful native language and then we anointed them with oil as a sign of the fresh anointing the Lord was pouring out upon them for breakthrough. As this was happening, the leaders across the room were encouraged to press into God and we experienced a very powerful time of deep prayer. I repented on behalf of Britain for releasing a dictatorial spirit into Uganda when we had colonised it and we closed the door to it. I found myself prophesying that something was shifting in Uganda and that Kony would no longer have the power that he had previously held. It was a new day for Uganda!

Many people were moved to tears and we could only imagine what this meant to those who were daily experiencing the hell of living with a tyrant like Kony and his army. The songs of praise and worship that followed were awesome and there was once again a real sense that something was shifting. A young man, who was a victim and then a part of Kony's army, sang about how God takes our mess and turns in into a message. Truly God was at work!

The climax of the conference was an amazing time of praise, worship and powerful intense prayer. Personally, I prayed in a way I had never prayed before with such a heavy burden for England and for my Church at home. Arnold asked Lee and I to speak at the end of the conference to draw it to a close. Lee got up to speak first and as he finished what he was saying, he jumped up on the table again. The Leaders loved it and were clapping joyfully. The next minute Lee grabbed my hand and pulled me up on to the table. The whole place erupted as I realised that God was probably laughing too!

We had bought two hundred Bibles with money we had brought with us. We were honoured to present Bibles (some in English and others in the local languages) to some of the Pastors who had been leading Churches without even possessing a Bible. For us that would be unthinkable and yet for them they had no choice. They clambered around us, hungry for the word of God and ready to devour every page. We came away with a heavy burden to raise enough money to be able to purchase and supply as many Bibles as we could. Over the years since that time, we have provided thousands of Bibles and teaching materials to help equip the Churches and their Leaders.

One new learning experience for us was visiting the toilets! They were in a block with a couple of cubicles for the ladies and a couple for the men. These were used by thousands of people on the site and the smell when you opened the door was challenging to say the least. There were no lights and you entered the cubicle knowing that once you shut the door you were in almost complete darkness. The toilet itself was a simple hole in the ground, and you had to ensure that you did not slip on anything and end up putting your foot down there. You did not know what could be lurking in the darkness and you really had to trust God. The ladies would go together (that is what ladies do!) and Anita would always lead the way. She had come prepared with a "Marks and Spencer" room spray. Anita would fling open the toilet door, put her hand inside, spray and then declare, "It is now safe for you to go in ladies!" She did make us laugh and you do have to see the funny side of these moments.

Another funny side of Uganda conferences can be the administration and the time. Time is so completely different and you have to learn to go with the flow and laugh at the delays and changes, or you would burst with frustration. The second year we visited Uganda, Graham, Sue, Hazel and Ruth had flown out a few days ahead of us to help on a Medical Mission. A couple of days before I was due to fly I received a phone call from them. They said, "You had better bring your robes out with you when you come!" The posters advertising the conference had been distributed everywhere and there was a slight mistake on the titles. The Conference was honoured to have a Baptist Archbishop from America speaking and everyone was looking forward to his arrival. However, the posters had photos of all the speakers including me and I had become Archbishop Sue Sinclair and the actual Archbishop had lost his title! I wonder if I was the first female Archbishop in the world? Actually I was quite embarrassed about it at the time, but everyone saw the funny side of it including the real Archbishop, which was a relief.

Back to our first visit - an opportunity arose for us to meet with Patience (President Museveni's daughter) but before we could do that we needed to be checked out. We went for lunch with Joseph, Patience's Secretary, before we could be granted permission to meet with her. The meeting went very well and Joseph promised to report favourably back to Patience.

While we were waiting for a decision, we went shopping for furniture for Abundant House. We bought some sofas, armchairs, a dining table, chairs plus a coffee table and several bunk beds. All the furniture was carved with elephants and giraffes, reminding us of our safari adventures.

Graham, Arnold and I were given permission to visit Patience at her home, which had a beautiful view overlooking Lake Victoria. Patience is a wonderful Christian woman who started a fellowship in her home. We had a good time with her and spent time praying and prophesying over her and her family. I shared the word the Lord had given to me while we were at the conference with the leaders. I prophesied that God was doing something very special in Uganda particularly relating to the removal of Kony and the foundations of the LRA. On the way back from Patience's home, we paused to grab some food at a local petrol station and I thought I heard a radio announcement relating to Alice Lekwina.

We drove on to KCC where we prayed for the plots laid out for houses six and seven. As we prayed for house seven we were amazed at the things God was showing us and we asked who would be raising the funds for this particular home? To our amazement we discovered that house seven was going to be funded by Brussels Vineyard Church! Arnold knew our wonderful friends Keith and Chris Sunderland, who Pastor Brussels Vineyard Church and Stephan Stouffs, a member of their congregation is the architect for KCC. What astonishing connections!

We then gathered together to dedicate Abundant House and I shared the scriptures from John 10:10 *"The thief comes only in order to steal and kill and destroy. I came that they may have and enjoy life, and have it in abundance (to the full, till it overflows)."*

What a great prophetic word to be declared over the precious children who would make Abundant House their home in the days ahead! We were then served goat BBQ and enjoyed a fantastic performance from the KCC choir.

Arnold, Graham and I then made our way to the home of Emmanuel who is the leader of the government's opposition party. Once again we had an awesome time of fellowship with him and his family, with an opportunity to pray and to prophecy over them and their nation.

Friday 19th January 2007 was our final day and we gathered together for communion and a time of powerful prophecy over our team. We then discovered that Alice Lakwina, who was in her fiftys, had suddenly died of a mystery illness the day before. She had become ill the previous Thursday afternoon (the day that we had prayed at Murchison). Alice was the founder of the Lord's Resistance Army, the former Ugandan rebel leader and self-declared prophetess. It was said that Joseph Kony and the Lord's Resistance Army drew their demonic powers through her.

Arnold then took us into the worst of the Kampala slums, which was one of the most horrendous things I have ever witnessed and experienced. It had rained heavily earlier in the morning and as a result the ground was very muddy. The tiny, poor quality, wood and tin shed homes were packed very tightly together in the midst of a river of mud and excrement. Each home housed huge families with lots of children, with no clean running water and no facilities.

Ann, a local minister led us into this community armed with pineapples, bananas and bread, we had bought earlier. We were instantly mobbed by dozens of starving adults and wide-eyed children from every direction. Yet in the midst of such extreme poverty, the men invited us in to smoke with them and partake of their hooch - we politely declined! A young boy begged us to visit his starving mother, who had literally just given birth to a stillborn baby. We felt so helpless and yet she was so thrilled to be visited by the Muzungos (white people). We were pleased to at least provide for their next few meals and to pray for them. Despite what we saw as a horrendous living environment, the children were full of joy and happy to play with pieces of string and old car tyres.

I felt ashamed that I was traumatized by simply passing through whilst for thousands of people this was their home 24/7. I have to be honest with you and say that I found the smells, the horrendous mud and the whole experience overwhelming and very intimidating. I wept all the way through the slums and did not stop until days after we returned home to Liverpool.

We waved farewell with lots of tears and our lives changed forever, having experienced more of God than we had ever known before and we were hungry to take that home with us.

A few days after we got home, we heard that the children had arrived safely in their new home Abundant House. There were five girls and four boys aged between two and ten; plus Peter (who has Downs Syndrome and had been abandoned in the slums some years earlier). We prayed for them to adjust to their new lives by settling in quickly and being healed from all the physical and emotional traumas they had endured. Rejoice and again I say rejoice!

Just one week after arriving home from Uganda I received a text from Arnold. As I read the text I was so shocked that I lost my ability to speak. The text said, "Uganda is still shaking from your prayers and now Kony's High Priest has also died". I was stunned that we had prayed and prophesied, and within two weeks two people had died! That was really scary and left me with such a burden to ensure we are very careful to only pray and prophecy what God tells us to. I must add we did not pray for them to die, as that would be witchcraft and that is not how God wants us to operate.

However, Uganda is changing and the lives of some of the most vulnerable people on the earth were redeemed from slavery, abuse, rape and murder. A short while later, we heard that many of Kony's men chose to lay down their weapons and walk away from him. After many months of trying to negotiate peace with the Ugandan government we heard that Kony had given up and left Uganda without most of his army. Thank God that a new day was dawning!

We have returned to Uganda many times since then and witnessed some wonderful things. Sadly, we have seen some horrific things too. One of the worst things I have experienced was a few years ago, when we were holding a conference in a huge dusty field. The conference was attended by 2,500 thousand leaders who had come from all over Uganda, Burundi, Kenya, Congo and Rwanda.

I had spoken and there was a huge response. Hundreds of people came forward for prayer ministry and each member of the ministry team had long queues of people patiently waiting for their turn. I had prayed for several people, when a woman with a young child in her arms reached the front of the queue. She had tears running down her face and I could see there was something clearly very wrong.

During our visits to Uganda we had seen thousands of women who could not look you in the eye. They would hang their heads in shame and they looked as though their bodies were still alive, but because of the trauma they had experienced the light of life had been extinguished. As I looked at this precious little girl in her Mummy's arms, I could see the same thing upon her.

I gasped and cried out to God to help me as I suspected what may have happened. The little girl was less than a year old and her Mummy told me in broken English, that her little baby girl was called Faith and she had been raped!

"No! No! No God!" I cried silently. Such anger rose up inside of me at the dreadful injustice and wickedness that crushes innocent lives. I knew that the African witch doctors have a lot of power and control over many of these communities. People cannot afford or do not have access to medical professionals so they go to the witch doctors for help. Many of the men who have contracted AIDs and HIV are told to go and have sexual intercourse with a small child and it will take away their diseases! The men are so deceived that they believe this is true and act on the instructions they have been given. It is horrendous to imagine what damage is done to these little children and what diseases they have contracted.

Meanwhile I was stood in this field, surrounded by thousands of people with this Mummy and her baby Faith. I took this beautiful little one in my arms and cried with her Mummy. Then I called on God and I pulled heaven to earth to do what I could not do. I prayed that God would completely heal Faith and restore everything to her and her Mummy that the enemy had stolen. I prayed that God would restore her to the destiny that He had for her. I came away with tears running down my face, my heart was breaking for this little family and many more like them. I do not get angry very often, but I came away furious that things like this are still happening and what was the Church doing about this?

I spoke to many of the Church Leaders and told them what had happened. They simply said, "Yes we know, these things happen all of the time!" Unbelievable! I took every opportunity God gave me after that to challenge the Leaders to rise up in prayer to see this practice STOPPED! They had incredible authority and they needed to use it.

So far I have not found out what happened to that precious little girl and her Mummy. Maybe one day I will meet them again and hopefully soon this horrendous act of witchcraft will be stopped.

Another little girl we were privileged to help was Deborah. Chris Wells and I had gone to a Church to preach, when we were invited to go into one of the local homes to pray for a child. When our eyes had adjusted from the bright sunshine, we saw hidden under the mosquito net, a little girl. She was whimpering and in terrible pain whilst her Mum watched helplessly.

In Uganda they do not have an environmental strategy and when they have any rubbish they simply throw it away or burn it. Every night there are fires burning across each community. The fires are not shielded or protected in any way and the children play around them, often unaware of the danger. It is common for the children to stumble and fall into the fires receiving major burns. There is no treatment for them, as their parents have no money to take them to the hospital and the medical care may be too far away for them anyway.

Deborah was only four years old and whilst playing, another child had pushed her into a fire. Now Deborah was lying naked on the bed; her little body was shaking and she had a high temperature. I am no medic but I could see that she had sustained very severe burns and she was very ill.

From the left side of her waist, I could see a huge raw burn, which spread across to the middle of her tummy and then right the way down her left leg. Her left arm and little hand also had horrible burns. I asked permission if I could go under the net to pray for Deborah and a moment later I was next to this precious little girl. Her huge tear filled eyes looked at me with desperation for her pain to stop.

"Lord, please help me, to help Deborah", I quickly whispered to God. I sensed that this was a life or death situation for this little one. I remembered I had a bag of baby wipes in my bag and I quickly took them out and put them on to Deborah's forehead to try to cool her down. I began to pray, breaking the power of the shock and trauma from Deborah's body, soul and spirit. I prayed for her full recovery and that she would not be robbed of her destiny. I commanded the pain and any infection to be gone. Then Chris and I emptied our purses and passed the money to her Mummy for her to be taken to the hospital.

We went home and raised £1000 to pay Deborah's medical bills, as she would need lots of surgery and skin grafts in the months ahead. Thank God, Deborah recovered fully and went on to live a normal life.

ISLE OF MAN

By 2007 we had delivered our four pieces of coal, experiencing the most incredible journeys and adventures with God. The stories of our trips to Stormont, Brussels and Washington DC had even reached the ears of Rowland Roderick in South Wales. Rowland was the man who had originally sent out the coal with the prophetic word. He rang me and we had a crazy chat on the phone about all the places to which the Welsh coal had travelled. He promised me I would receive a margarine tub in the post in the next few days.

A brown parcel arrived as expected and I wondered what I would discover when I unwrapped it. To my surprise, inside the tub was a further supply of coal, twenty-seven pieces to be exact. Oh my goodness what was I going to do with those?

Earlier in the year Norma Dean had met David Talbot from the Isle of Man. Having heard the stories of the pieces of coal he was keen to receive one for his island. As soon as we realised we could provide a piece of coal to the Isle of Man, we contacted David and arranged for some of our team to fly over.

We arranged to arrive the day before Tynwald Day[1] on 5th July 2007. The flight from Liverpool was only a few minutes long and the team of eight of us; Norma Dean, Ruth Dyke, Jan Cornish, Rosemary Dagger, Jean Dodd, Anita Gowan, Doreen Kelly and I arrived on a beautiful sunny morning. As we walked from our aircraft across the tarmac we walked straight into our first divine appointment!

The timing of our flight was perfect. As we disembarked from our little plane, we were greeted by the Minister of Tourism. She was actually waiting to welcome David McClarty, who was the Assembly Member from Northern Ireland, off his flight - he was the man who took us around Stormont. David was a guest for the Tynwald Day and his flight was due a few minutes after ours had landed. She welcomed us to the Isle of Man and when we told her why we were visiting, she invited us to attend the official opening of the new Viking Centre in Douglas. I found myself warmly accepting the invitation on behalf of our team and hosts. Our hosts, who had lived in the Isle of Man all their lives, commented that a member of the government had never invited them to anything!

David and Ravina Talbot gave us a very warm welcome and we were taken to meet their local Christian community. After lunch we visited the Tynwald Hill, the location for the annual Tynwald Day open-air meeting of the Isle of Man's parliament. The four-tiered hill is man made, stands 72 feet high and is a distinctive landmark. The open-air ceremony includes a reading of all the laws that have been passed throughout the year and always takes place on 5th July. Tynwald Day was established by Norse Viking settlers over a thousand years ago and remains a highlight of the island's activities.

We were informed that we would not be able to get anywhere near Tynwald Hill as the security would be so tight as they prepared for the big day. However, as we arrived we chatted with the staff who were busy assembling marquees and laying out chairs, and they were happy for us to climb the hill to pray.

We left Tynwald Hill to visit the Tynwald Building, the permanent home for the Isle of Man government located in Douglas. We were thrilled to be welcomed by Edward Crowe (Minister from the Legislative Chamber), David Anderson (Minister from the House of Keys), the Chaplain and a Tour Guide. Edward and David told us they could only give us five minutes of their time as they had a lot of preparation to do for Tynwald Day. They took us up to the top of the building that overlooked Douglas and the Lord said, "I want you to pray for them here". We had a powerful time with them there and we sensed God's presence with us very powerfully. Interestingly, they remained with us until the end of the tour almost two hours later.

Anita said, "I have been praying prior to coming on the trip and the Lord told me that the piece of coal was to be deposited in a table". We did not know where that table would be, but as we entered the central chamber, over an hour into the tour, Anita nudged me. She whispered to me that the table in the centre of the room was the table she had seen in the vision from God. Oh my goodness! I wondered how on earth could I explain this to Edward, David and the others, if I did not fully understand it myself? In the end I decided that if they thought I was completely mad it would not matter, as they would probably never see me again, but I could not disobey God.

So I took a deep breath and began to speak, trying to give a plausible explanation about the coal. Thankfully God goes ahead of us and He had prepared the way for the arrival of this piece of coal too. I asked their permission to pray as I placed the piece of coal on the highly polished table. I prayed, asking God to pour out His blessing upon them, their government and their nation. After I had finished praying, Edward was wide eyed and asked if he could hold the coal. He said it was the most beautiful coal he had ever seen and then he began to explain why the coal had to go in that exact place on that particular table.

The Isle of Man Parliament is the oldest in the world and apparently they used to meet in a circular building where the fire was located in the centre of the room. Historically the sword, which dates from approximately the

15th Century, was used to stoke the fire and to this day the tip of the sword is fire damaged. The Tynwald Parliament is not constituted properly without the ancient Sword of State that usually sits on the table. Amazingly the tip is always positioned exactly where I had placed the coal. However, this day it was away being polished in preparation for Tynwald Day, as it is used to lead the Lieutenant Governor and the Government out on to the hill.

Edward then asked what was going to happen to the coal. I glanced across at David Talbot and he nodded approval to me to use it as I felt the Lord was leading. I said I was not sure yet where God wanted us to leave it. Edward asked if we would be willing to deposit the coal in the drawer under the table. What a great idea! So our little piece of coal remained and was deposited in the drawer under the ancient Sword of State in the oldest Parliament in the world. How amazing is that?!

If that were not enough, David then asked if I would like to see the replica sword that is kept hidden away. Did I want to see it - of course I did! They pulled out the replica and I got to hold that for a few precious moments of prayer.

Before we left they asked if we were planning to attend Tynwald Day. We told them that we were and when we told them where we would be sitting they said "Oh no, those seats are not good enough for you!" They honoured us by giving us the best tickets for the day.

We left the Tynwald Building and made our way to the Viking Centre just a few blocks away. People dressed as Vikings greeted us and as we entered the auditorium we wondered what we had agreed to come to. There was a band on the platform playing Viking music as they announced they were awaiting the arrival of the First Minister, Tony Brown who had got stuck in heavy traffic.

I looked at Norma and she was sprinkled with gold dust, all over her black trousers and her hands. I had none! However, I recognised that the gold dust was a sign from God that something was about to happen and we needed to be ready. A little while later the First Minister arrived to officially open the Centre and then we were invited to attend a special VIP reception with the First Minister! I waited my opportunity and when Tony Brown was about to walk past me, I greeted him and told him we had come from Liverpool to pray for him and his government. I had a few moments with him to hear what he wanted us to pray for and to bless him. Make sure you are ready for the divine appointments that God brings your way.

We arrived to take up the seats we had been given and were invited to receive some weeds that everybody seemed to be wearing on their lapels. We declined the offer but people all insisted that we should wear it. We asked people why they wear it, but most people did not know anything more than this was the custom on Tynwald Day and everybody had to wear it. Eventually somebody told us they wore it to appease the gods - what!

Often we come under traditions without having any idea of what we are tying ourselves into. I was glad that we had decided not to accept the lapel weeds. We sat and watched the final preparations and listened to the Church Service that was being conducted in St John's Church at one end of the path. Workers were busy distributing bundles of rushes to appease the sea god Manannan, before the church service finished. The person making the announcements proudly declared that this was a Pagan and Christian event as the procession of people led by the very polished Sword of State left the Church. People were dressed for a wedding with the men in top hats and tails, and the ladies dressed in high heels, beautiful gowns and stunning hats. They all walked along the path over the rushes to take their positions on Tynwald Hill. When everyone had taken their seats, the government began and law was passed for the next year. We prayed and had opportunities to pray for several people there.

We had further opportunities to meet with some wonderful people and to share God's word with them. God met with us all very powerfully and we give Him glory for all that He did there.

[1] http://www.tynwald.org.im/about/tynday/Pages/default.aspx

REPUBLIC OF IRELAND

Graham and Sue Derrig were invited to take a team to the Republic of Ireland in September 2007. Anita Gowan, Norma Dean, Liz Boote, Angela Roberts and I joined them on this particular adventure.

A couple of years before, we had hosted our wonderful prophetic friend, Martin Scott. He prophesied over Norma that she would be going back to visit her Celtic roots in Ireland. Not long after that Kathie Walters posted something on the Elijah List that was all about St Patrick and his time in Ireland. Norma heard the Lord tell her to print all seven pages out and put them in a drawer safely, as one day she would need them. Months went by, in fact a couple of years and Norma had totally forgotten all about it.

We were preparing for our trip when Norma suddenly had an urge to clear out her drawer full of papers. As she looked through them Norma came across the document all about St Patrick, and felt that she needed to pack that in her bags for the trip. Norma read it through again and as she did, realised that it was a blueprint for our visit to Ireland. On the short flight Norma passed it to Graham to read and then on to me. The document talked about Patrick arriving in Ireland and being accompanied by Victor who said he was the Angel of Ireland. As they journeyed together miracles broke out everywhere they went.

On 10th September we landed at Dublin Airport with trumpets sounding because the flight had arrived a couple of minutes early; that really made us laugh, as we had never had trumpets sounding our arrival before. We found the mini-bus we had hired and made our way to the hotel. After unpacking, we were joined by John, a friend of Graham's, and walked along to Trinity College that was located just along the road.

On the way we noticed a tiny traffic island in the centre of the road, with four trumpeters facing North, South, East and West. Liz and Angela had brought their shofars with them (a huge musical instrument made from rams horn and used by ancient Israel to make announcements), so they crossed over onto the island and began to blow. As they did this the rest of our little team stood on the pavement and prayed for the wind of the Holy Spirit to blow through the land once again. Then something crazy and unexplainable happened, suddenly out of the sky dropped a croissant! What on earth did that mean? It missed hitting us by a couple of inches and landed on the floor.

We continued on into the grounds of Trinity College and entered the Chapel to pray. We decided to allow the Holy Spirit to guide us in where we needed to go to pray. As we stepped back out into the bright sunshine my eyes were drawn to the NIKH building opposite. This was the post-graduate reading room and also a war memorial to the 463 men who had died during the Great War. NIKH is the name of the Greek goddess of victory. It was interesting that Norma and Graham were also drawn to this building and we were the only ones who had read the document about St Patrick and the angel Victor.

We began to pray and I felt God was empowering me to close down the power of NIKH. We did not want to see people engaging with a false victory - we wanted the best for the people who found themselves studying at Trinity College. So I began to pray but I could hardly stand up. I felt really dizzy, nauseous and it felt as if my jaws had been wired together. Despite this I knew I needed to keep praying and it meant that Graham and Norma literally had to hold me up to keep me standing. I finished praying and called upon the angel Victor to return to the land. Thankfully, the burden then lifted from me.

The Book of Kells, a 9th century gospel manuscript, famous throughout the world, was housed just around the corner in the Old Library. It was a massive attraction and crowds of people were queuing up to pay ten Euros to go in. A lovely lady appeared asking if we wanted to see it, so Graham and I opted to go in on behalf of the team. This precious lady led us in past all of the people queuing and right into the room. I was overwhelmed by people's hunger to see the Word of God, and yet realising that many people would have Bibles sitting on their shelves gathering dust.

We came out of the Old Library and joined the rest of the team ready to leave the grounds of Trinity College. As we came around the corner, back into the main square in front of the NIKH reading room Anita let out a loud shriek. We turned to her and she was as white as a sheet. She told us she could see a giant angel, twenty-five feet tall standing in the centre of the square overlooking the NIKH reading room. He stood with his arm raised high holding a large sword aloft and declared, "My name is Victor and I am here to stay!"

Nobody else saw Victor the angel. The fact that Anita saw Victor was so encouraging to us, as she did not know the story of Victor, she was not present when we had prayed and called for Victor's return. The other incredible thing was that Anita had never seen an angel before either!

We left Trinity College totally overwhelmed by what God had done and expectant of more. We walked a few blocks to the Irish Houses of Parliament, which meet in the Dail Eireann building. Graham had contacted them prior to our trip asking permission for us to go in for a visit, but they had refused. We arrived at the entrance to be told that it was closed to the public. However we have learned by now that if God wants us to go in somewhere, He will open the door for us no matter what men may say.

We explained to the receptionist that we had come from Liverpool especially to pray God's blessing upon the government. Moments later we were invited to sit on a bench in the reception area while we waited for our Tour Guide. Yeah God! As we waited, I heard the Lord whisper to me to anoint my hands and to pass the bottle of anointing oil between the team. I wondered what was going to happen next. What did God have planned?

Suddenly a smartly dressed lady arrived and greeted us warmly. She was our Tour Guide who had been brought through especially as the building was closed to the public. She started by leading us through the large double doors towards a beautiful, wide white marble staircase. She was very chatty and informative as we made our way up the stairs.

A gentleman appeared and began to make his way down the stairs and our Guide introduced him as the Communities Minister. He was warm and friendly, quickly reaching out to shake my hand, which of course was covered in anointing oil. As we explained why we were there, he did not attempt to remove his hand from mine. I asked him if we could pray a blessing upon him and he was thrilled. We encountered three Government Ministers in that way and we shook hands with every one, anointing each one with oil as we prayed for them.

We will probably never know what God has done in their lives or through their lives as a result of those encounters. It does teach us not to accept "No" for an answer when you know that you have heard from God.

The following day we drove to a place with a very bloody past, Drogheda, located on the West Coast of Ireland. This is a land that suffered three sieges in the 17th Century. The first was in December 1641 and the second was 11th September 1649. Here we were exactly 358 years to the day following the second siege. 1649 was famous because it was the siege laid by Oliver Cromwell and it is reported that approximately 2,500 and 10,000 people died, depending upon whose historical report you are reading. The third siege was the Battle of the Boyne in 1690 and named after the River Boyne that runs through Drogheda. We spent some time praying there.

We also visited the Hill of Tara and the Hill of Slane. The Hill of Tara was the ancient inauguration site of the high Kings of Ireland. It was said that St Patrick defeated the power of the Druids here. The Hill of Slane can be seen from Tara, and was notably the place where St Patrick lit the first paschal fire in direct defiance of the pagan Kings nearby.

We left this beautiful nation knowing the Lord had been with us and that we had completed all that He had called us to do.

WINDSOR CASTLE

Norma Dean and I were invited to stay at Windsor Castle in September 2009 to be a part of a prayer summit. Well as you can imagine we jumped at the opportunity and were thrilled to be staying in such an amazing place.

Windsor Castle is actually the oldest and largest occupied castle in the world and is the Official Residence of Her Majesty the Queen. It has a rich history that spans almost 1000 years, covers an area of about thirteen acres and overlooks all of Windsor. It is also the home of St. George's Chapel where ten previous Monarchs have been buried.

You are not allowed to park in the Castle grounds due to the high security. So we parked my car in one of the public car parks at the bottom of the hill and we walked up to the entrance with our suitcases. Well actually, I hobbled up the hill as I had sprained my ankle a few days earlier. I had a big suitcase with a little sword in, as Norma had heard the Lord tell her to bring it. I also had my shofar packed in the bag, as I knew that was going to be important. We had to show our passports for the police to allow us to enter, but they did not check our bags and we did not think about the potential consequences of taking a sword into Windsor Castle.

It was a beautiful day as we gathered together with friends from across the nation to pray for Her Majesty the Queen and our nation. We heard from several people throughout the day and spent some time praying. It was incredible to realise afresh the spiritual responsibilities that Her Majesty Queen Elizabeth carries on behalf of our nations and the nations of the Commonwealth. Not only that but she has the final responsibilities for the Government, for the Church of England, the Armed Forces and so much more. I am so pleased that she is such a Godly and righteous woman.

God showed us that we were in an incredible place where three spiritual cords are entwined together - those that hold the earthly government, those that hold the sovereign government and those that hold the spiritual Church government. The Lord said there had been a pull on each of those cords to disconnect them from each other and to pull each one apart.

Scripture tells us that a three-stranded cord cannot be broken. The Lord has certainly had His hand upon this relationship for His plans and purposes. The Lord said *"If you choose to put your hands on each of these cords, not only will you pick up the anointing God desires to pour out through the earthly government, the sovereign government and the church – you will also release the power of God which will shake and shake to bring release and the restoration of God's purposes. Are you willing and are you prepared to allow God to pour into you and through you, these different anointings? These anointings will break off the old mantles and yokes to usher in the new, for those who are open to receive."*

We were told that at 10.30pm, when all the tourists would be gone and the work of the day finished, we would be given a Guided Tour of St George's Chapel. The Lord whispered to me that He wanted me to blow the shofar there. In St George's Chapel at 10.30pm at night - surely not! After all, Her Majesty the Queen could be in bed with her rollers in! No, that could not be right, but cnce again the Lord said *"I want you to blow the shofar in St George's Chapel"*. I told Norma and she agreed that it sounded like something God would say. "Oh rats", was my reply! I was not very confident at blowing the shofar. Many people cannot even get a sound out of it at all, and for me it only makes a sound when the Holy Spirit enables.

I made a million excuses why I could not do it. I told the Lord I would not be allowed to blow it. *"Ask the Tour Guide,"* the Lord whispered. The very smart Tour Guide arrived and looked like she would definitely not entertain the idea of anyone making too much noise in the Chapel. "Lord she will say No!" I whispered in utter terror. *"Ask her,"* the Lord urged me. So I took a big deep breath and asked her, "Would it be possible for me to blow the shofar in the Chapel?" "Yes that will be fine," she said to my amazement.

Oh no, that was not the reply I wanted. I was intimidated by the others in the group and could just see myself blowing the shofar and this little squeak coming out. I was allowing the fear of man to control me big style! I decided that this Tour Guide would forget all about me and my shofar, so I would not have to blow it. However, God was determined that this shofar needed to be blown and our lovely Tour Guide led us informatively around the Chapel, stopping at the bottom of the aisle that leads all the way through the main Chapel to the Altar. She suddenly turned to me and said "This would be a great place for you to blow your shofar."

I thought I was going to faint, as I panicked but Norma was busy praying for me. What would I do without her? I looked around at the group who were all looking at me in expectation. "I am not very good at blowing the shofar," I blurted out "If anyone else knows how to blow this, please feel free to come and blow it." There was complete silence and nobody stepped forward. So I had no choice but at least to try. I was praying desperately and completely depending on God as I raised the shofar to my lips, took a deep breath and blew.

The most amazing sound came out of the shofar, filling the whole of the Chapel and echoing into every corner and crevice. It seemed to last for a very long time as God kept filling my lungs with His breath. As I finished the Lord said, "Do it again". So I breathed in again and blew. Again the same sound filled the entire place and left my body vibrating with God's power. As the sound ebbed away the Lord whispered once more, "Do it again". So for the third and final time I breathed in deeply and released the sound. It felt as though the whole atmosphere had changed, but was I just being dramatic?

That night we slept in the grounds of Windsor Castle in St George's House. Our room was lovely and we had a beautiful gift of Molton Brown toiletries waiting for us. Despite the room being very comfortable I struggled to sleep. I am blessed to sleep really well at home or when I am travelling in our nation or abroad. However, this particular night was different, as I continued to feel the sound reverberating through my body until morning. As I lay awake the Lord whispered to me again, *"My eyes are upon your nations and when the Changing of the Guard happens at 11am go and watch it, pay attention and I will speak to you."*

THE CHANGING OF THE GUARD

Windsor Castle is guarded by the resident regiment of Foot Guards from the Household Division in their full-dress uniform of red tunics and bearskins, accompanied by the Guards' Band. The Changing of the Guard ceremony encompasses forty-five minutes of spectacular colourful pageantry that has taken place almost every day since 1660. This all takes place in the Castle Forecourt and draws tourists from all over the world. As you can imagine it is an amazing sight to see and to hear, and certainly not one to miss!

The person speaking in our first session finished a few minutes after 11am, but Norma and I ran out of the room to take our place ready for God to speak to us. We positioned ourselves to watch outside the guardroom, by Henry VIII's gateway, as the process of the guards transferring the keys was performed.

The old guard, the new guard and the band were all in position at the same time. The Lord said, *"This is a time of transition where there is a doubling of the watchmen and the guard!"* As we arrived, the guards all stood positioned, quiet, listening and alert, waiting for the next command and the instructions to come. The Lord asked, *"Who do you think will issue the command?"* I wondered if it would be the Conductor of the Band or one of the Sergeants of the old or the new guard. However, the silence came to an end, as the Officer with the largest base drum issued the commands to bring a shift of officers. Officers moved around, and then the band struck up a song before coming to a silent pause again, listening for the next command.

To our left the general public watched shuffling about and talking amongst themselves, unaware of the significance of what was playing out before them. The Lord said *"Many across the Church are just like that and have a unhealthy disregard of the transition set before them, of the times and the seasons that we are living in and the urgency of the hour."*

The silence was broken once again when the drummer issued the command, and this time the Sergeants from the old guard and the new guard walked to the centre of the parade ground. They began to march together perfectly in step, shoulder to shoulder, with their highly polished swords drawn. They then paraded from one side to the other. Amos 3:3 says *"Do two walk together unless they have agreed to do so?"* Those who were about to march out, and those who were about to take their posts, walked together for a few moments, shoulder to shoulder! Then the band struck up a song once again, and began to march out of the parade ground with the old guard following them out. This completed the changing of the guard and left the new guards to take their place - spot on time!

Then the Lord said:

"As a group of nations you are in a time of huge transition. The old guard and the new guard are both in the same place at the same

time. The old guard is ready to move on or be moved on to make room for the new."

"The pages of the history of your nation are about to be turned; the pages that represent the Government, the Monarchy, and the Church. There is a frustration in those positioned, waiting to move into place, but their timing, although almost upon them, is not quite here. There are many spectators in each of these three areas who do not perceive the radical shift about to come."

"The pages of the history of your nations are about to be turned but the pages that represent the Government, the Monarchy and the Church have not yet been written. What would you have me write upon them?"

How could God possibly ask us? After all He was the one who created the heavens and the earth and who knows all things. Why would He ask us? Just like Esther was asked by the King, "What would you have me decree for you?" The Lord was saying, *"What would you have me write upon the pages of the history of your nations?"* We had an opportunity, whilst there was still time, to effect what would be written!

We set about mobilising people to pray for the Government, the Monarchy and the Church. We listened carefully to God and we began to declare a time of massive shifting over the Government, the Monarchy and the Church. We knew that the next General Election was due in May 2010, eight months away, and could be a really major opportunity to see the Government shift dramatically. Like many other ministries, we really encouraged Christians all over the nation to pray for the election. We began to see that there was going to be Coalition Government.

THREE SHIFTS

FIRST SHIFT – THE GOVERNMENT

After thirteen years with a Labour-led Government, the UK went to vote on 6th May 2010. As we had expected, the General Election resulted in no clear winner and it was left to the Conservatives, who had won the most seats, to form a coalition government with the Liberal-Democratic party. The leaders, David Cameron and Nick Clegg, were forced for a season to walk together shoulder to shoulder for the sake of the nations, even though on many issues they see things from very different perspectives. Since that time there has been a huge and speedy shift taking place... some good and some not so good!

I am not a party political person but I do have a great passion to see God's government functioning here on earth. The governmental shift had started and since then has impacted every sphere of life. So far the shaking has caused major cutbacks affecting services across the Local Authorities, Police Authorities, Health Authorities, Fire Authorities, the Armed Forces and every other part of the public sector, including the voluntary sector. Some things did need to change, as we could not continue to spend money that we did not have. However some of the cuts that have been made have been brutal, leaving some people with nothing and having to turn to Food Banks to even have something to eat.

THE BIG PUSH

Since 2009 our CWM team has been leading the Big PUSH once a month. This is a gathering of Christians coming together who love to praise, worship and pray with a passion and hunger to see heaven touching and impacting earth. The Big PUSH has been a very significant journey for Christians from across the Mersey Region, as we have been learning to PUSH into the presence of God together.

We gather people who are from different styles and families of Church, choosing to gather together to praise, worship and cry out to God for the release of a major move of God once again within our land.

This is what one person said, "I have been refreshed, healed, uplifted, empowered and most of all I have grown closer and more intimate to God. The times of worship have been incredible and at times I have really felt I was in the throne room of God."

Another said, "What a meeting! It is so hard to put into words, when you meet with the living, almighty, all powerful, incomprehensible God. His presence was so tangible, even as I entered the room. It was certainly a throne room experience!"

Another said, "Good to be at the Big Push yesterday, God quietened me with His love and I could feel His presence; a healing balm in the midst of the shaking going on."

As well as individual people being touched by God, heaven has touched earth in many other ways too. The Big PUSH in December 2010 was one of those occasions. We were just about to take the offering when God spoke,

"When you take the offering, everything that is left over after you have covered your costs, I want you to give towards the national debt!"

This was one of those moments when you shake your head, because you question if you have just heard correctly. So I said, "What Lord?" Again the Lord repeated the clear instructions, so as Norma was just about to take the offering I told her what the Lord had said.

After we had taken our expenses out, we rounded the money up to £400 and wrote a cheque out to Her Majesty's Government. Shortly before we flew out to Uganda in January 2011, I wrote to Prime Minister David Cameron enclosing the £400 cheque, saying, "If Prime Minister David Cameron would receive this cheque as a seed towards the national debt, God would multiply it." What an opportunity, I wondered what God would do.

MULTIPLICATION CAN IMPACT

We flew out to Uganda and experienced something amazing as God miraculously multiplied our money twice. You cannot get a supply of Ugandan Shillings whilst in the UK, so we have to arrange for our money to be exchanged when we are in Uganda. You get a much better exchange rate the more money you have to exchange, so when going to Uganda our whole team puts all our money together and then we divide it all up again after it has been changed. We had two people in the team responsible for the money. They counted all of the money as they received it from the team and counted it again before putting £7,050 into the bag to take it to the Money Exchangers. They removed the money from the bag and gave it to the Money Exchangers who counted it using an automatic counter twice and by hand once. The money had increased to £7,110 an extra £60!

When they calculated our exchange it gave us 28,750,000 Ugandan Shillings. This money was brought out of the safe in three bundles of ten million shillings, bound and certified by the Bank of Uganda. They gave us two bundles of 10 million, and opened the third, from which we watched them count and remove 250,000 shillings. Then they counted the money across the counter and a few minutes later, three people including the member of staff from the Money Exchangers, counted the Ugandan Shillings back into the bag.

We made our way back to our Bed and Breakfast in Kampala, and the two members of the team responsible for the Ugandan Shillings began to count the money out of the bag. Then they counted it again, as they were amazed to see it had increased again by an extra 140,000 shillings. How good is that? Thank you Lord!

We were all in awe because we knew this extra of 400,180 Ugandan Shillings meant we could release more resources to make a powerful difference in people's lives. As you can imagine that is a lot of money in Uganda.

There have been generations of families affected by domestic violence, even amongst Church Leaders in Uganda. I was challenged to speak to the Leaders at the Conference to stop the violence and to renew their marriage vows afresh. Then, because we had received the extra money, we were able to sow 4,280,000 Ugandan Shillings into a new ministry about to launch to help resolve marriage and family problems.

God is in the multiplying business! In Genesis 1:28 God told Adam and Eve, to be fruitful, multiply, and fill the earth, and subdue it, using all its vast resources in the service of God and man. I am certain that does not just mean have children – it means everything that is good we can multiply!

Returning from Uganda, we were very confident that God was good at multiplying money. We received a letter from the Prime Minister's Office saying that they could not receive the cheque and hoped we could find a good cause to give it to. How many of us give up at the first disappointment?

God had said we were to give it and we were not prepared to accept a NO, even if it had come from the Prime Minister's Office. God had said we were to sow the money into the national debt and we had a responsibility to make sure that happened. On 16th March 2011 we visited the Houses of Parliament to meet our MPs and ask them how we could give our £400 towards the national debt? They were more than a little surprised and eventually told us that there was no protocol in place for this money to be paid against the national debt. We realised that we were about to bring breakthrough!

We were not willing to go back home to Liverpool with the cheque, so later that same day we walked into the Treasury. The Treasury is located very close to the Houses of Parliament and as we entered the building we were reminded that this was one week before the next UK Budget would be announced. As we entered the Reception area the Holy Spirit came with us. People began to smile and laugh - people do not usually do that in the Treasury, especially the week before the national budget! The Holy Spirit began to touch people and they began to laugh.

We explained that we had come from Liverpool to pay some money off the national debt. They did not know what to do with us, as there was no system in place for people to do that! The men on reception began to make frantic phone calls and sometime later we spoke to Sir Nicholas MacPherson, the second most powerful British civil servant. We told him that if the Treasury would receive this money, we believed that God would multiply it. He told us that this money would have to be shown on the Government budget documents, as it did not fit into any other category! So our little £400 was shown on the national budget! Sir Nicholas sent a young man down to the reception to receive the cheque. The young man smiled as he received the £400 and told us he would arrange for us to receive a note to acknowledge the receipt of the money. God gave us a prophecy for this young man, a Christian, who was so encouraged!

Five days later, on Monday 21st March, Norma rang to say that the BBC news headline was "Budget 2011: Government due £8 billion windfall". They actually announced that the Treasury had found £8billion they did not know they had! That is a multiplication of 20 million from our little £400! That's our God - He is awesome! He cares about our nations. Just imagine how many jobs, may have been saved by that money.

As if that were not good enough, a few days after the Budget we received a hand written envelope containing a hand written note from the Chancellor of the Exchequer, George Osborne himself (a copy of the letter is at end of book). We photocopied this letter and gave a copy to everyone who had given into the offering in December, just to encourage them to see what God can do when we are simply obedient.

SECOND SHIFT – THE MONARCHY

As soon as we knew we were going to London, Norma wrote to The Very Reverend Dr John Hall, the Dean of Westminster Abbey since 2006. Norma asked him if we could go into the Abbey to pray for the Government, the Monarchy and the Church. Westminster Abbey is the place where our Monarchs are crowned, where they make promises to God on behalf of our nations and, very often where they are married. It is a very powerful place and was already in the midst of busy preparations for the wedding of Prince William to the very beautiful Kate Middleton.

Whilst at a CWM meeting one morning, Norma missed a personal phone call from The Very Reverend Dr John Hall himself. He left Norma a lovely message on her answer phone, saying that he was really excited that we wanted to come to pray, and that his secretary would be in touch soon with the arrangements for us to go in as his guests, instead of paying £18 per person admission charge. We thanked God for His favour upon us.

After our meeting with our MPs in the Houses of Parliament we walked across the road and into the very imposing Westminster Abbey. We had been invited to enter through the "Great West Door", which is the entrance used at all official events, and not the entrance used by tourists. As we entered a loud voice over the PA announced, "We particularly wish to welcome the Community Watchmen Ministries Team into Westminster Abbey today." Wow, we were not expecting that and we felt that it was as if God was saying *"You have my permission to do what I need you to do here!"*

We were warmly greeted by one of the Canons, who then introduced us to one of the Vergers, who would give us a personal Tour of the Abbey and answer any of our questions. The tour was brilliant as there is so much history within the confines of this incredible building.

We asked if we could pray in the places that Prince William and Kate would be throughout their wedding ceremony. We were privileged to enter the area containing the Shrine of Edward the Confessor. This is not usually an area open to the general public and is a place in history of very significant private meetings. This included the meeting on 17th September 2010 when the Archbishop of Canterbury, Rowan Williams prayed privately with Pope Benedict XVI. We did not know this at the time, but this was the place where Prince William waited for his beautiful bride to arrive. Later the bridal party entered this area away from the prying eyes of the press and public to sign the wedding register.

I was led to read this scripture calling for the dry bones of the Government, the Monarchy and the Church to arise as a mighty army.

"The hand of the Lord was on me, and he brought me out by the Spirit of the Lord and set me in the middle of a valley; it was full of bones. He led me back and forth among them, and I saw a great many bones on the floor of the valley, bones that were very dry. He asked me, "Son of man, can these bones live?" I said, "Sovereign Lord, you alone know." Then he said to me, "Prophesy to these bones and say to them, 'Dry bones, hear the word of the Lord! This is what

the Sovereign Lord says to these bones: I will make breath enter you, and you will come to life. I will attach tendons to you and make flesh come upon you and cover you with skin; I will put breath in you, and you will come to life. Then you will know that I am the Lord." So I prophesied as I was commanded. And as I was prophesying, there was a noise; a rattling sound, and the bones came together, bone to bone. I looked, and tendons and flesh appeared on them and skin covered them, but there was no breath in them. Then he said to me, "Prophesy to the breath; prophesy, son of man, and say to it, 'This is what the Sovereign Lord says: Come, breath, from the four winds and breathe into these slain, that they may live." So I prophesied as he commanded me, and breath entered them; they came to life and stood up on their feet - a vast army." Ezekiel 37

As I was reading these verses and prophesying, God took me back many years to a powerful vision He gave me. I was in a dark place that reminded me of the terrible gas chambers that the Jewish people were led into within the concentration camps during the World War II. The walls were dark grey concrete and there were no windows. The door had been closed and locked. There was no natural light but there was a narrow beam of sunlight coming through a small gap in the ceiling behind me. As my eyes adjusted to the darkness I could see that the floor was covered with bones, all separated from one another and scattered covering every square inch of the concrete.

In the vision, I took a deep breath and the Lord told me to begin to walk amongst them. I began to walk and experienced such an anointing of authority and power to call these bones back to life. I was not afraid or anxious that I was on my own in a dark room full of dead bones. I knew that I was about My Father's business.

Back in Westminster Abbey I knew that prophetically, I was calling the scattered bones of the Government, the Monarchy and the Church to arise. I could see them beginning to shake and shift into position. Everything was changing but little did we know what God was about to do.

I was so focused on what I was prophesying, that I had forgotten the dead bones of so many Kings and members of the Royal Family surrounded us. Just around the shrine are the tombs of Henry III, Edward I, Edward III, Richard II with his Queen Ann of Bohemia, plus there are many more bones around the Abbey.

As I was declaring and prophesying these scriptures, a member of our team, Jean Dodd said, "If these bones start rattling I am out of this place!" We all laughed. I love that we can be doing the most serious things and yet we never take ourselves too seriously. I am not sure what the Verger thought about it all!

We left the shrine and positioned ourselves near to the altar. It was a very powerful time as we prayed for Prince William and Kate, as they were preparing for their wedding on 29th April 2011, only a few weeks later. We were informed of the exact location where they would stand to make their wedding vows and I fell to my knees on the ground. I repented on behalf of the Church that was born out of a desire of Henry VIII to get rid of his wife. We broke any curses, which may have come upon the Royal family and their marriages. We anointed the ground where Prince William and Kate would marry and released the blessing of God upon the royal family. We asked the Lord to bless their wedding day with real joy.

The Royal wedding was a joyful day, and after all the guests had left Westminster Abbey, the cameras filmed a member of the clergy doing cartwheels along the red carpet - his joy was clearly uncontainable!

The shift in the Monarchy had begun and on 17th May 2011, we had another significant sign of the shift. After a century of bloodshed, distrust and uneasy coexistence, with a great deal of love and hate along the way, the Queen opened a new era in the history of relationships with the Republic of Ireland. She proclaimed it not with a speech or a grand political gesture, but with a bright green hat and coat. Queen Elizabeth filled the most extraordinary gap that no politician had been able to fill, as she placed a regal foot on Irish soil. This was not merely a personal first for her, as no monarch has been there for one hundred years since King George V had said farewell in 1911.

Early June 2012 marked the start of Queen Elizabeth's Diamond Jubilee celebrations, 60 years since she became Queen. As part of the celebrations on 27th June 2012 Queen Elizabeth made a groundbreaking visit to Northern Ireland. Thousands of people lined the streets to welcome the Queen and Prince Philip to Enniskillen, the scene of one of the worst atrocities of the Troubles, when an IRA bomb killed eleven people on Remembrance Sunday in 1987. They attended a service to mark the Queen's 60th anniversary. The Queen's itinerary also included a brief meeting with former IRA leader and Northern Ireland's Deputy First Minister, Martin McGuinness. Queen Elizabeth's own cousin Lord Mountbatten was killed when an IRA device exploded on a family boating trip. As they shook hands she had to put aside her personal pain to stand in the gap for peace and reconciliation.

The 2nd June 2013 was sixty years since the Queen's Coronation and 22nd July 2013 saw the arrival of Prince William and the Duchess of Cambridge's first child, who is now third in line of succession to the throne.

Each Christmas Day the Queen makes a speech to the nations and her speeches in the last few years in particular, have been so full of the power of the Gospel. On Christmas Day 2012, she said: "This is the time of year when we remember that God sent his only son to serve, not to be served. He restored love and service to the centre of our lives in the person of Jesus Christ. It is my prayer...that His example and teaching will continue to bring people together to give the best of themselves in the service of others."

Most recently she said, "For me the life of Jesus Christ, the Prince of Peace, whose birth we celebrate today, is an inspiration and anchor in my life."

What an amazing woman of God!

THIRD SHIFT - THE CHURCH

Early in 2012 the Lord told us to pray for the new Archbishop of Canterbury. We wondered if the Archbishop of Canterbury, Rowan Williams even knew he would be leaving. The Lord said that *"The appointment of the new Archbishop of Canterbury would mark the start of the shift in the Church."* Now we all agreed that this sounded exciting and we set about praying.

In August 2012, an excavation began in a Leicester City Council car park. A skeleton of dry bones was discovered, believed to be King Richard III who had died in battle in 1485, 528 years earlier. On 4th February 2013, after many months of DNA testing, it was announced that the skeleton was indeed King Richard III. The dry bones of the royal family have certainly arisen!

Prophetically, vehicles mean ministry. The Lord said that this was a very prophetic picture where many ministries had come to a stand-still and were no longer moving in alignment with God's plans and purposes. The car park was dug up and the bones are being raised. The spine of the skeleton found was clearly very deformed. God said *"He is raising up the Church in this hour and re-aligning the spine to give the Church a new strong backbone and a powerful clear voice."*

On the same day as the DNA results were announced on the bones, the Right Rev Justin Welby, aged 57, took part in a service called "the Confirmation of election", becoming the 105th Archbishop of Canterbury. As the Archbishop of York declared Justin's name, he called him "Justice Portal Welby". We were certainly very excited to see Justin become the next Archbishop of Canterbury, as we had met him during his time serving as the Dean of Liverpool Cathedral. He is a good man and a mighty man of God.

We were thrilled to see a shift in the Anglican Church that we know will impact many nations. We thought that was it, but then on 11th February 2013 Pope XVI suddenly and unexpectedly resigned. The whole world was shocked, as he was the first Pope to do this in over six hundred years. That night lightening struck the Vatican - when a heart is out of rhythm an electric shock is required for the brain and the heart to start again in alignment. Was God shocking and shifting the heart of the Church?

We believe Pope Benedict had been listening to God and had been led by the Holy Spirit. During his time as Pope he led the way in repentance for the past sins of the Catholic Church and gave opportunities for those who had been hurt to be healed. He made way for a new move of God in and through the Catholic Church.

The magnitude of this Church shift is bigger than we could have ever imagined. These two men, leaders of the biggest Churches across the planet, both resigned and their replacements both started within a few days of each other. A portal certainly opened and we see the Church poised for a major breakthrough of the KINGdom of heaven to earth.

In Liverpool we have two Cathedrals, one for the Church of England community and the other for the Catholic community. On 7th January 2013 the most Reverend Patrick Kelly, Archbishop of Liverpool, announced his decision to retire after suffering a slight stroke. Then on 28th January 2013 the Bishop of Liverpool, James Jones, disclosed his intention to retire on his 65th birthday in August. Liverpool was certainly reflecting what was happening in the wider picture.

We have seen the three shifts begin and they have been so much bigger than we could ever have expected. This has released a season of multiplication and acceleration with lots of suddenlies! In this season the King, the Lion of the Tribe of Judah, is coming through the gates of heaven, looking for those who will partner with Him to serve His purposes. We need to determine to be a people who build the Kingdom and not just our ministries or Churches.

Let us align ourselves with God's plans and purposes, give thanks to God and give Him all the glory!

COASTLANDS & GATEWAYS

In Merseyside over the years, we have journeyed with the Lord and learned to operate as prophetic Watchmen, watching and praying protection over our region. As we have done that we have experienced a whole new level of protection and transformation. We have been able to thank God for his favour and security as we have witnessed several potential disasters disarmed.

Here are just a few examples:

1. A Merseyrail train running at peak time with 119 passengers on board derailed in October 2005, without anyone being killed or seriously injured. [1]
2. The landmark Liverpool Pier Head landing stage capsized into the River Mersey 2nd March 2006, without anyone falling into the sea or being injured.[2]
3. Two vessels collided in the middle of the River Mersey in thick fog on 3rd February 2007. The Alaska Rainbow cargo vessel hit the Isle of Man Seacat carrying 274 passengers, tearing a large hole in the hull of the Seacat. The hole caused water to pour into the engine room and yet all

of the passengers escaped safely – How amazing is our God![3]

4. 15th May 2006 the Royal Navy discovered an unexploded World War II 500kg bomb on the riverbed. The bomb was lifted off the riverbed and floated right over both Mersey Tunnels and the underground train tunnel, out into the Irish Sea before it was detonated.

5. On top of all of that there was a very near miss of two aircraft over Liverpool's John Lennon Airport.

We quickly realised that God takes our prayers seriously and particularly when we love the land and the people who live there. God recognises and responds to our passion and His compassion operating through us.

God has a habit of taking me by surprise and this was one of those times. I had a sense of the urgent need to establish a network or a linking together of people who lived or worked in gateway places. If God could provide a strong shield of protection over Liverpool, surely He could protect our nations too? A praying friend, Val Baskerville, a Bible Teacher and local Preacher in the Methodist Church from Ulverston, Cumbria, had a similar vision for the coastland areas and agreed to join forces with me to see what we could do.

I spoke to Martin Scott, who was someone I trusted to give me some guidance, and he was very supportive. Val and I agreed to invite a few friends from around the nation, to gather together to listen to God. We were sure that the Holy Spirit would have a strategy to enable us to do that and to establish further prayer protection for our nations.

In advance of this gathering, a few of us decided to visit the Western Approaches in Liverpool. You will recall this is the War Rooms where they co-ordinated the vessels at sea during World War II. I rang to see if we could bring the group into the Western Approaches to pray and was told by the Manager that they would be thrilled to welcome us. She told us that during the war it had been a place where people had prayed with great passion, as they understood that lives depended on God's strategies and intervention. Prayer was essential during the war, and as we entered the War Rooms there was an incredible sense of God's continued presence and power. Sometimes there are anointings from God deposited in places because of their history. We sensed that there was certainly a strong anointing present that we were determined to pick up. If we needed an anointing for spiritual warfare, this was one of the places where we could receive it. We had a powerful time of prayer and certainly received a fresh impartation for raising up the watchmen.

We decided not to send out any posters or leaflets, but to simply send out an email laying down what the Lord had placed on our hearts. We invited people to come along and to bring others they knew, who should be joining us on the journey.

We had expected a gathering of around thirty people, but we suddenly found over one hundred and twenty people responding to the email. In fact people joined us from all around the nations of the British Isles. We were thrilled to have many denominational prayer leaders and networks leaders represented. Some of the national Prophets also joined us to help us to hear what God was saying. This was a unique gathering of people who had never all been in the same place, at the same time before. We enjoyed being together in God's powerful presence and it felt like a very strategic time.

Thursday 27th September 2007 happened to be National Maritime Day and this was the day we launched this new International prayer initiative, 'Coastlands and Gateways'. This gathering was a response to the need across the nations of the UK to have a pro-active prayer strategy in place across the networks, able to quickly mobilise effective prayer when required, e.g. when there is a sense of an impending terrorist threat or natural disaster. It is a call to rise up and stand as watchmen and gatekeepers, and to pray using the authority we have been given by God.

Val and I hosted the launch day in Liverpool with the help of Jenny and Steve Watson, Maria Fox, Phil and Anjie Gregg. Leaders from all across Scotland, England, Wales, Northern Ireland, the Republic of Ireland, Jersey and the Isle of Man joined us.

It was an exciting day, starting with a time of repentance and communion led by Brian Mills from Interprayer. I honour Brian for the many years he served our nation as part of Billy Graham's UK team. Brian had also received an important prophetic word about raising up people to pray around the coasts.

We shared how God had given the vision to raise up a protective prayer shield around the nations. Later we received prophetic input from Martin Scott, Sharon Stone, Rachel Hickson and Sue Mitchell. We finished with a powerful time of commissioning, led by Arnold Muwonge. There was a great sense of this being a very strategic prayer initiative birthed by the Holy Spirit.

We have only mobilised this prayer network when there has been a real threat to life. One of the first times we mobilised, was in the winter of 2007, when there was a huge threat of the East coast being flooded and many lives lost. Thousands of people were evacuated from their homes as they waited for the impending disaster to strike. Suddenly, during the night the wind changed direction and the expected flood did not materialise.

Since that time it has been mobilised only two or three times a year, and we can really thank God that there has not been a successful terrorist attack since we have been praying. We do not take that for granted and we encourage people to keep praying. Our God is really awesome!

1. http://news.bbc.co.uk/1/hi/england/merseyside/4383540.stm
2. http://www.ldcc.org.uk/01764_02032006_The_sinking_feeling_on_the_River_Mersey.htm
3. http://news.bbc.co.uk/1/hi/england/merseyside/7015705.stm
4. http://news.bbc.co.uk/1/hi/england/merseyside/4988294.stm

SHOCKING TRUTH

One of the greatest breakthroughs we have seen relates to the shroud of death that was over Liverpool, resulting from the Hillsborough disaster. We believed the Lord said *"When death was lifted off Liverpool, revival would come".*

So we prepared ourselves to stand in the gap in prayer until the breakthrough came. After visiting the Heysel and Anfield football Stadiums, we felt that we needed to complete the journey with a prayer trip to the Hillsborough Stadium, so we waited for God's timing.

Through the years that followed there has been a cry for justice from the hundreds of families, friends, neighbours and colleagues who lost precious people on that day. People who had simply gone out for the day to enjoy a great football match and never came home again. A cry for justice from the survivors who have lived crippled lives physically, emotionally and spiritually ever since. Justice was not granted and there has been a gaping wound left in many, many lives. We knew that there was a powerful cover up and that was very hard for people to come to terms with.

As a team we try to support the G8 in prayer. In 2005 we spotted an opportunity to stand with Christians in Sheffield, as the Justice Ministers of the G8 were visiting in advance of the G8 meeting in Scotland. Was it a God incidence that we were going to pray in Sheffield (the home of the Hillsborough Stadium) in preparation for the arrival of the most powerful JUSTICE Ministers in the world? We knew we had stepped into a divine appointment prepared by God in answer to our prayers. We had come to support the G8, but we had also come to pray in Hillsborough to see TRUTH, JUSTICE and forgiveness released. We wanted to see healing and breakthrough come, as we believed that when the earth reflects what is happening in the heavens, there is an opportunity for us to call for justice.

We spent the morning in prayer with our friends from Sheffield. Then someone said we needed to move the group to the General Cemetery to pray after lunch. Now I do not know what you think about that, but we thought it was really weird!

This place had been closed since the 1970's, was completely overgrown and used for all kinds of witchcraft, pagan worship, rapes and right in the middle of it all is a Buddhist peace garden. We walked and prayed around the cemetery for a while. To be honest it all seemed a bit irrelevant to the G8 Justice Ministers visit. We had finished walking around when someone appeared and gave us an information brochure for the cemetery. The back page included details on a paupers' grave that was the deepest and largest paupers grave in the UK. This grave held the bodies of 96 people, which happened to be exactly the same number of people who had died at the Hillsborough Stadium!

What happened next was so unexpected. Norma was reading aloud the details about the unmarked paupers' grave when the Spirit of God suddenly fell heavily upon us. We were doubled over, gasping and crying out, weeping in deep intercession, releasing forgiveness and calling for a breakthrough for Liverpool and for Sheffield.

We left the General Cemetery, inviting those from Sheffield to come with us to the Hillsborough Stadium, but nobody wanted to. The steward was lovely, taking us into the Leppings Lane area, the site of the crushing and leaving us there to pray. I found it very hard to breathe, as I could almost hear the screams and see the men, women and children as the life was being crushed out of them. We sat in the area where they had breathed their last breaths and we cried out to God for breakthrough to come. We felt like tiny little people facing a huge Goliath, BUT we knew we had God on our side! We prayed through Lord Justice Taylor's Interim and then Final Reports, that had been set up immediately after the disaster. We released truth and forgiveness to every person and organisation mentioned plus any other people that we knew of.

Finally we asked if we could go to see the memorial stone. Apparently the families of those who had died there in Hillsborough, had fought for ten years before Sheffield Wednesday had agreed to allow a memorial stone to be laid there at all. The Steward led us right out of the Stadium to the area where the memorial stone was located. We were shocked to see that just like the paupers' grave there were no names. It was as though all those men, women and children's lives counted for nothing - they were just nameless, faceless people, not even important enough to have their names recorded.

We continued to pray, looking to the Lord to see what He would do as we completed that stage of the stadium journeys from Heysel to Anfield and on to Hillsborough.

THE JOURNEY TOWARDS THE TRUTH

The 15th April 2009 marked the 20th Anniversary of the Hillsborough disaster. Twenty years of trauma and heartache. Twenty years of people fighting the system to see truth and justice come. Twenty years of disappointments and discouragements. However, it had also been twenty years of standing together shoulder to shoulder. As usual the families and survivors held a memorial service in the Anfield Stadium. However, that year over 30,000 people turned up to the largest Church service in the nation. People came from miles around and even the media came along to broadcast it live on Sky News, the BBC and other channels.

My husband, Steve and I went along too and as we walked into the stadium alongside hundreds of other people, we could tangibly feel the deep, deep pain. People walked in complete silence, lost in their memories and the trauma of that day and the aftermath, but determined to stand together.

The strength of people's hurt and frustration with the legal system had not dissipated at all. The thirty thousand people present were only a token of the number of people who would have been there if they could - some had to work or some simply were still too traumatised to face it. For those who did, it was a very powerful gathering. In the midst of the service, Andy Burnham MP came out to speak on behalf of the Government. Before he managed to get into the flow of his speech, people began to stand all across the stadium. 30,000 people standing together, from different football teams, different walks of life, different cultures and different geographies, standing shoulder to shoulder, to release a huge, united deep, deep cry of "Justice for the 96" again and again. The tears of a city with a broken heart flowed and the sound touched heaven and went all around the world. Andy Burnham stopped speaking until the crowd had finished and was clearly moved.

We were told later, that Andy Burnham went back the next day to see Prime Minister Gordon Brown and put Hillsborough back on the agenda for the Cabinet meeting that day.

Sheffield and Nottingham also held Memorial Services and kept the two minute silence while many stood in silent tears. This was not a Liverpool disaster, but a national disaster made so much worse by the lies and the deception. Truth and justice were required and we were as determined as the families and survivors that the breakthrough would definitely come.

CALLING FOR THE TRUTH

We waited for God to signal the right time to follow this through to breakthrough. When he did, I called together a small team of people I trusted, including Steve Lowton, Brian Mills, Gill Birtill, Lynda Yoxen and Jane Holloway, to represent the nation; Norma Dean and I representing Liverpool plus Tony Canning who is both a Hillsborough survivor and a serving Merseyside Police Officer; Ruth Bussell and Kay Wainman representing Nottingham; Baz Gascoyne and John O'Brien representing Sheffield, plus the Chaplain of Sheffield Wednesday and Maria Fox, representing the Police.

We met together on 7th July 2009 in Sheffield where we once again visited the General Cemetery and the Hillsborough Stadium. The weather was appalling, as though the angels were weeping and we all got soaked to the skin! The weather did not stop us, as we had come too far now to stop. We gathered together in the Leppings Lane end of the stadium, which was a really momentous thing for all of us, but especially for Tony who had not been back since that fateful day on 15th April 1989.

Tony was a young man on that day and had gone to stand alongside his best friend, to enjoy a great football match. Tony came home, but his friend never made it back and like many other survivors, Tony had lived his life ever since, riddled with survivor guilt that he should never have had to carry. We had a very powerful time of prayer and really sensed that breakthrough was on its way.

I was really thrilled, when we did not have to wait too long. Just a few weeks later on 29th July 2009, the Home Office announced its commitment to release all of the information that had not previously been made available. They also declared their intention to appoint an Independent Panel to oversee the release of the information. Wow, we knew this was the start of the wall of deception and lies being demolished and we really thanked God.

We began to pray for the people who would be on that Independent Panel, as it would be completely useless if the wrong people were appointed. Then on 26th January 2010 the Independent Panel members were all appointed. The Panel was led by our wonderful Bishop of Liverpool James Jones and included:

- Phil Scraton, Professor of Criminology from Queen's University in Belfast and author of Hillsborough: The Truth.
- Katy Jones, TV and factual producer on Jimmy McGovern's Hillsborough.
- Peter Sissons, TV Broadcaster.
- Raju Bhatt, Legal Expert.
- Christine Gifford, Government Adviser on the disclosure of highly sensitive materials.
- Dr Bill Kirkup CBE, who was Regional Director of Public Health.
- Paul Leighton CBE QPM, who retired as a Deputy Chief Constable in Northern Ireland and served on Her Majesty's Inspectorate of Constabulary (HMIC), where he assisted in the inspection of a number of English police forces.
- Sarah Tyacke CB, who was a Keeper of Public Records and was responsible for the establishment of The National Archives in 2003.

We spent many hours within the next thirty-two months praying for the Independent Panel, as they poured through thousands of documents. We prayed particularly for Bishop James, who sadly suffered serious heart problems requiring surgery part way through.

The Panel's role was to ensure that the Hillsborough families and the wider public received the maximum possible disclosure of all relevant information relating to the context, circumstances and aftermath of the tragedy. They had the very difficult and painful job of researching and analysing the documents, and then providing a comprehensive report. I wondered if this had broken Bishop James's heart?

For the first time in a very long time the families of the deceased and the survivors began to feel they were being listened to. Although they still doubted there would be any breakthrough, as they had been disappointed so many times before, but could this be the time when the tide would begin to turn?

On 17th October 2011 the House of Commons hosted another debate led by Steve Rotherham, MP for Walton, Liverpool. This was amazing and groundbreaking for a number of reasons. First of all a change was made to enable people to request a debate in Parliament. This would be approved if they got more than 100,000 people to sign an E-Petition on the Government's new E-Petition website. Most people had not factored for the level of support this petition would get, as within days it had passed 138,000 signatures and the debate was approved.

I clearly remember sitting on my living room floor watching the debate, which was live on Sky TV. The debate went on for hours, as one after another, MPs arose to identify themselves with the families and survivors. The speeches were passionate and emotional and once again it felt like another brick in the wall was being dismantled. I wrote to every single MP to thank them for their contribution and to encourage them to continue their support until the truth and justice had come. I received a personal response from each MP assuring me of their continued support.

Meanwhile the Independent Panel actually did an amazing job and managed to produce the report without any leakages to the press or media. The families of the ninety-six were invited into Liverpool Cathedral on 12th September 2012, to be the first people to hear the Report. Not even the Prime Minister or the Government had seen it prior to the families.

We knew the date for the Report to be released 12/9/12 was very significant as the number 12 is for government and 9 is the time of new birth!

I sat praying for Bishop James and the Panel members as they reported to the families. I prayed for the families as they listened to the worst possible truth that proved they had been right all along. I prayed for them as they discovered that the truth was actually much worse than they could have ever imagined. The families were given some time and support to begin to take in what they had been told.

Meanwhile a press conference was assembled, and before anything was said the reporter from The Sun newspaper was asked to leave. Members of the Panel were seated in the Lady Chapel of the Cathedral and began to speak to the world's media. I sat weeping uncontrollably, like many, completely aghast as the report was much worse than any of us could have imagined. Calmly, Bishop James led the panel as they disclosed some of the most shocking truths that had ever been disclosed. These are just a few of the points made:

1. The Report cast doubts over the original Inquests ruling, revealing that at least 41 of the 96 victims 'had the potential to survive.' What! How on earth were the families going to cope with knowing that their son, daughter, father, brother or friend could have survived if they had been given the right help in time?
2. South Yorkshire police and emergency services made 'strenuous attempts' to deflect blame for the crush onto victims. This was done to endorse the lies the police were telling to deflect the blame on to the supporters.
3. 116 of the 164 police statements were amended to remove or alter comments that were unfavourable to South Yorkshire police.
4. Police carried out blood alcohol readings on victims, including children, in order to 'impugn their reputations.'

Now most of the facts are known, and I suggest that for further understanding of just how dreadful this disaster and its aftermath was, you read either of the publications below for yourself:

Professor Phil Scanlon's excellent book - "Hillsborough the Truth" or "The Hillsborough Disaster Independent Report"[1]

After years of battling the system and praying, suddenly within a couple of hours, everything had changed. Immediately, people were queuing up across the nations to give their apologies; including Prime Minister David Cameron who made a complete and profound apology in Parliament for the 'double injustice' of the Hillsborough disaster. I make no apologies for including this in its entirety as we had been praying and waiting for twenty-three years for it to come. These are the words of Prime Minister David Cameron to the House of Parliament.

"The disaster at the Hillsborough football stadium on 15 April 1989 was one of the greatest peacetime tragedies of the last century. Ninety-six people died as a result of a crush in the Leppings Lane Terrace at the FA Cup semi-final between Liverpool and Nottingham Forest.

There was a public inquiry at the time by Lord Justice Taylor, which found, and I quote, that the main cause of the disaster was "a failure of police control". But the inquiry didn't have access to all the documents that have since become available. It didn't properly examine the response of the emergency services. It was followed by a deeply controversial inquest and by a media version of events that sought to blame the fans.

As a result, the families have not heard the truth and have not found justice. That is why the previous government, and in particular, the Rt Hon Member for Leigh was right to set up this panel. And it is why this government insisted that no stone should be left unturned and that all papers should be made available to the Bishop of Liverpool and his team.

Mr. Speaker, in total over 450,000 pages of evidence have been reviewed. It was right that the families should see the report first. As a result, the government has only had a very limited amount of time to study the evidence so far. But it is already very clear that many of the report's findings are deeply distressing.

There are three areas in particular. The failure of the authorities to help protect people. The attempt to blame the fans. And the doubt cast on the original coroner's inquest. Let me take each in turn.

First, there is new evidence about how the authorities failed. There is a trail of new documents, which show the extent to which the safety of the crowd at Hillsborough was "compromised at every level". The ground failed to meet minimum standards and the "deficiencies were well known". The turnstiles were inadequate. The ground capacity had been significantly over-calculated. The crush barriers failed to meet safety standards. There had been a crush at exactly the same match the year before. And today's report shows clearly that lessons had not been learnt.

The report backs up again the key finding of the Taylor Report on police failure. But it goes further by revealing for the first time the shortcomings of the ambulance and emergency services' response. The major incident plan was not fully implemented. Rescue attempts were held back by failures of leadership and co-ordination. And, significantly, new documents today show there was a delay from the emergency services when people were being crushed and killed.

Second, the families have long believed that some of the authorities attempted to create a completely unjust account of events that sought to blame the fans for what happened. Mr. Speaker, the families were right.

The evidence in today's report includes briefings to the media and attempts by the police to change the record of events. On the media: several newspapers reported false allegations that fans were drunk and violent and stole from the dead. The Sun's report sensationalised these allegations under a banner headline, "The Truth". This was clearly wrong and caused huge offence, distress and hurt.

News International has co-operated with the panel and, for the first time, today's report reveals that the source for these despicable untruths was a Sheffield news agency reporting conversations with South Yorkshire police and Irvine Patnick, the then MP for Sheffield Hallam.

The report finds that this was part of police efforts, and I quote, "to develop and publicise a version of events that focused on... allegations of drunkenness, ticketlessness and violence."

In terms of changing the record of events, we already know that police reports were significantly altered but the full extent was not drawn to Lord Justice Taylor's attention. Today's report finds that 164 statements were significantly amended and 116 explicitly removed negative comments about the policing operation, including its lack of leadership.

The report also makes important findings about particular actions taken by the police and coroner while investigating the deaths. There is new evidence, which shows that police officers carried out police national computer checks on those who had died in an attempt, and I quote from the report, "to impugn the reputations of the deceased."

The coroner took blood alcohol levels from all of the deceased including children. The panel finds no rationale whatsoever for what it regards as an "exceptional" decision. The report states clearly that the attempt of the inquest to draw a link between blood alcohol and late arrival was "fundamentally flawed". And that alcohol consumption was "unremarkable and not exceptional for a social or leisure occasion".

Mr. Speaker, over all these years questions have been raised about the role of the government, including whether it did enough to uncover the truth. It is certainly true that some of the language in the government papers published today was insensitive. But having been through every document and every government document including cabinet minutes will be published, the panel found no evidence of any government trying to conceal the truth.

At the time of the Taylor Report, the then Prime Minister was briefed by her private secretary that the defensive and I quote "close to deceitful" behaviour of senior South Yorkshire officers was "depressingly familiar". And it is clear that the then government *thought it right that the chief constable of South Yorkshire should resign. But as the Rt Hon Member for Leigh has rightly highlighted, governments then and since have simply not done enough to challenge publicly the unjust and untrue narrative that sought to blame the fans.*

Third, and perhaps most significantly of all, the Bishop of Liverpool's report presents new evidence, which casts significant doubt over the adequacy of the original inquest. The coroner, on the advice of pathologists, believed that victims suffered traumatic asphyxia leading to unconsciousness within seconds and death within a few minutes. As a result he asserted that beyond 3.15pm there were no actions that could have changed the fate of the victims and he limited the scope of the inquest accordingly.

But by analysing postmortem reports the panel have found that 28 did not have obstruction of blood circulation and 31 had evidence of heart and lungs continuing to function after the crush. This means that individuals in those groups could have had potentially reversible asphyxia beyond 3.15pm in contrast to the findings of the coroner and a subsequent judicial review. And the panel states clearly that "it is highly likely that what happened to those individuals after 3.15pm was significant" in determining whether they died.

Mr. Speaker, the conclusions of this report will be harrowing for many of the families affected. Anyone who has lost a child knows the pain never leaves you. But to read a report years afterwards that says, and I quote, "a swifter, more appropriate, better focused and properly equipped response had the potential to save more lives" can only add to the pain.

It is for the attorney general to decide whether to apply to the high court to quash the original inquest and seek a new one. In this capacity he acts independently of government. And he will need to examine the evidence himself. But it is clear to me that the new evidence in today's report raises vital questions, which must be examined. And the attorney general has assured me that he will examine this new evidence immediately and reach a decision as fast as possible. But ultimately it is for the high court to decide.

It is also right that the house should have an opportunity to debate the issues raised in this report fully. My Rt Hon friend the Home Secretary will be taking forward a debate in government time. And this will happen when the house returns in October.

Mr. Speaker, I want to be very clear about the view the government takes about these findings and why after twenty three years this matters so much, not just for the families but for Liverpool and for our country as a whole.

Mr. Speaker what happened that day and since was wrong. It was wrong that the responsible authorities knew Hillsborough did not meet minimum safety standards and yet still allowed the match to go ahead. It was wrong that the families have had to wait for so long, and fight so hard, just to get to the truth. And it was wrong that the police changed the records of what happened and tried to blame the fans.

We ask the police to do difficult and often very dangerous things on our behalf. And South Yorkshire police is a very different organisation today from what it was then. But we do the many, many honourable police men and women a great disservice if we try to defend the indefensible.

It was also wrong that neither Lord Justice Taylor nor the coroner looked properly at the response of the other emergency services. Again, these are dedicated people who do extraordinary things to serve the public. But the evidence from today's report makes very difficult reading.

Mr. Speaker, with the weight of the new evidence in this report, it is right for me today as prime minister to make a proper apology to the families of the 96 for all they have suffered over the past 23 years. Indeed, the new evidence that we are presented with today makes clear that these families have suffered a double injustice. The injustice of the appalling events; the failure of the state to protect *their loved ones and the indefensible wait to get to the truth. And the injustice of the denigration of the deceased, that they were somehow at fault for their own deaths.*

On behalf of the government and indeed our country, I am profoundly sorry for this double injustice that has been left uncorrected for so long.

Mr. Speaker, because of what I have described as the second injustice, the false version of events, not enough people in this country understand what the people of Merseyside have been through. This appalling death toll of so many loved ones lost was compounded by an attempt to blame the victims. A narrative about hooliganism on that day was created which led many in the country to accept that it was somehow a grey area. Today's report is black and white. The Liverpool fans "were not the cause of the disaster".

The panel has quite simply found "no evidence" in support of allegations of "exceptional levels of drunkenness, ticketlessness or violence among Liverpool fans", "no evidence that fans had conspired to arrive late at the stadium" and "no evidence that they stole from the dead and dying".

Mr. Speaker, I'm sure the whole house will want to thank the Bishop of Liverpool and his panel for all the work they have done. And I am sure that all sides will join with me in paying tribute to the incredible strength and dignity of the Hillsborough families and the community, which has backed them in their long search for justice.

While nothing can ever bring back those who have been lost with all the documents revealed and nothing held back the families, at last, have access to the truth. And I commend this statement to the house."

Even a certain newspaper printed the real TRUTH although not many people in Liverpool bought copies. The apologies were helpful but the people of Liverpool could not celebrate, as the truth was so deeply shocking. The lid had come off and people found it very difficult to know how to deal with their emotions. There was great sadness, because many family members and survivors had died or committed suicide, unable to carry the burden any longer, before they had heard the truth or seen justice come. Many marriages and relationships had been shattered and lost, as people could not deal with the trauma effectively.

However the truth has helped as the Home Secretary announced a new Police inquiry into the disaster. There was some pleasure on 19th December 2012 when the High Court quashed the original inquest verdicts of accidental death, as the Lord Chief Justice ordered fresh inquests. He said:

"The combination of circumstances, as we have narrated, makes inevitable the order for a new inquest. The interests of justice must be served. Within the limits of the coronial system, the facts must be investigated and reanalysed in a fresh inquest when, however distressing or unpalatable, the truth will be brought to light. In this way the families of those who died in this disaster will be vindicated and the memory of each victim will be properly respected... All the inquisitions will be quashed. There will be new inquests in each and every case."

A group came together made up of footballers, Managers and recording artists, including Sir Paul McCartney, Robbie Williams, Kenny Dalglish and many others, to record a charity song called "He ain't heavy, He's my brother". It sold 269,000 copies and made it to No.1 in the charts. Through this song money was raised to support the families in their legal journey towards justice. To be honest every time I heard it, the tears would flow.

At the time of writing, the new Coroners Inquests are now underway. The Rt Hon Sir John Goldring was appointed as the Assistant Coroner for South Yorkshire (East) and West Yorkshire (West) to conduct the inquests. They are being held in a purpose-built courtroom, the biggest in England and Wales, located in Warrington.

The Inquests started 31st March 2014 and are not expected to be finished for some time. Unlike the first inquests, the families of the 96, were each allowed to give a personal statement about those loved ones they had lost at Hillsborough. These statements, as you can imagine, were the first real opportunity for anyone to hear about the precious people who died on that day. Many people have already been called to give evidence – Police Officers, Emergency Service Officers, players, survivors and many others.

Wednesday, 11th March 2015, was a very significant day in the Hillsborough Inquests and happened to be the day I attended with Liam Moore. The Court Room was packed tight full of the families of those who had died and members of the press. This was because it was the second day that David Duckenfield was giving evidence. He was the Chief Superintendent responsible for the policing of the Hillsborough Stadium on that awful day in 1989.

During questioning by QC Christina Lambert, David Duckenfield eventually admitted that he had lied, after he gave the order for the gates to be opened, and that he had no idea where those two thousand people would go when they came through. He also admitted that he had given no instructions prior to the gates being opened, to close the tunnel, to avoid more people entering the already over full central pen area.

A few days later, he admitted the failure to close the tunnel into the central pen *"was the direct cause of the deaths of ninety-six people".*

Suddenly, later in the afternoon when confronted that he had lied, David Duckenfield turned towards the families of the bereaved and said: *"I apologise unreservedly to the families."* He continued *"Everybody knew the truth, the fans knew the truth and the police knew the truth, that we had opened the gates."* David Duckenfield, now aged 70, said *"He would regret the lie to his dying day".*

Later he said:

"What I would like to say to the Liverpool families is this: I regret that omission, and I shall regret it to my dying day. I said something rather hurriedly, without considering the position, without thinking of the consequences and the trauma, the heartache and distress that the inference would have caused to those people who were already in a deep state of shock, who were distressed, and for them to find out in a way that, because of my, shall we say, candid behaviour, which is expected of a senior officer, I had heaped upon them what's, shall we say, further damage when they had got problems enough."

The people of Liverpool had waited almost twenty-six years to hear those words. Gasps could be heard all around the court and many tears flowed that day, including mine. One precious man who had lost his brother at Hillsborough, later said to us, that he felt like a huge weight had been broken off his chest. The shroud of death was beginning to be lifted off.

There are further shocking revelations almost every day, as people are being called to give evidence who were not called during the last inquests. Two witnesses have spoken of at least two of the most senior Police Officers being members of the same Freemasons Lodge. In fact David Duckenfield confessed to being the Grand Master!

The Police involved in the Hillsborough disaster and the aftermath are now being investigated, and time will tell of the outcomes. We are praying that there will be no scapegoats. We give thanks to God for the TRUTH that has come and is still coming. Having released forgiveness, we continue to look to God, for mercy to triumph over judgment and for healthy justice to come.

Finally, in this chapter I want to say how much I honour and thank God for some of the people in this journey:

- The families and survivors who have fought tirelessly for the truth to be exposed especially – Margaret Aspinall CBE, Trevor Hicks CBE and the amazing Ann Williams who died a couple of days after the 24th anniversary before she could attend her son's inquest.
- The people of Liverpool and fans of Liverpool FC who have stood together and never given in.
- Liverpool FC – particularly:
  - Kenny Dalglish, who ceaselessly continues to support the families.
  - Steven Gerrard whose ten-year old cousin was the youngest person killed at Hillsborough.
  - Rafa Benitez who continues to support the campaign for justice.
- The MPs of Merseyside and beyond who have done their best to bring breakthrough.
- The members of the Hillsborough Panel and their staff.
- Jimmy McGovern who made a very thought provoking and factual TV film about the disaster.
- Many others behind the scenes who have never let this go.

1. http://hillsborough.independent.gov.uk/report/Section-1/summary/

WE WILL REMEMBER

I also want to honour those who never came home:

John Alfred Anderson (62)

Colin Mark Ashcroft (19)

James Gary Aspinall (18)

Kester Roger Marcus Ball (16)

Gerard Bernard Patrick Baron (67)

Simon Bell (17)

Barry Sidney Bennett (26)

David John Benson (22)

David William Birtle (22)

Tony Bland (22)

Paul David Brady (21)

Andrew Mark Brookes (26)

Carl Brown (18)

David Steven Brown (25)

Henry Thomas Burke (47)

Peter Andrew Burkett (24)

Paul William Carlile (19)

Raymond Thomas Chapman (50)

Gary Christopher Church (19)

Joseph Clark (29)

Paul Clark (18)

Gary Collins (22)

Stephen Paul Copoc (20)

Tracey Elizabeth Cox (23)

James Philip Delaney (19)

Christopher Barry Devonside (18)

Christopher Edwards (29)

Vincent Michael Fitzsimmons (34)

Thomas Steven Fox (21)

Jon-Paul Gilhooley (10)

Barry Glover (27)

Ian Thomas Glover (20)

Derrick George Godwin (24)

Roy Harry Hamilton (34)

Philip Hammond (14)

Eric Hankin (33)

Gary Harrison (27)

Stephen Francis Harrison (31)

Peter Andrew Harrison (15)

David Hawley (39)

James Robert Hennessy (29)

Paul Anthony Hewitson (26)

Carl Darren Hewitt (17)

Nicholas Michael Hewitt (16)

Sarah Louise Hicks (19)

Victoria Jane Hicks (15)

Gordon Rodney Horn (20)

Arthur Horrocks (41)

Thomas Howard (39)

Thomas Anthony Howard (14)

Eric George Hughes (42)

Alan Johnston (29)

Christine Anne Jones (27)

Gary Philip Jones (18)

Richard Jones (25)

Nicholas Peter Joynes (27)

Anthony Peter Kelly (29)

Michael David Kelly (38)

Carl David Lewis (18)

David William Mather (19)

Brian Christopher Mathews (38)

Francis Joseph McAllister (27)

John McBrien (18)

Marion Hazel McCabe (21)

Joseph Daniel McCarthy (21)

Peter McDonnell (21)

Alan McGlone (28)

Keith McGrath (17)

Paul Brian Murray (14)

Lee Nicol (14)

Stephen Francis O'Neill (17)

Jonathon Owens (18)

William Roy Pemberton (23)

Carl William Rimmer (21)

David George Rimmer (38)

Graham John Roberts (24)

Steven Joseph Robinson (17)

Henry Charles Rogers (17)

Colin Andrew Hugh William Sefton (23)

Inger Shah (38)

Paula Ann Smith (26)

Adam Edward Spearritt (14)

Philip John Steele (15)

David Leonard Thomas (23)

Patrik John Thompson (35)

Peter Reuben Thompson (30)

Stuart Paul William Thompson (17)

Peter Francis Tootle (21)

Christopher James Traynor (26)

Martin Kevin Traynor (16)

Kevin Tyrrell (15)

Colin Wafer (19)

Ian David Whelan (19)

Martin Kenneth Wild (29)

Kevin Daniel Williams (15)

Graham John Wright (17)

WALKING WITH LIONS

God had been speaking to us for a long time about going to South Africa. It was as though the Lord Himself had put South Africa right inside our hearts.

At our monthly Big PUSH gatherings we welcome many special guests from across the UK and the nations. We had some wonderful visitors arrive from South Africa, Cheryl Moskos and her husband Gary Smythe. We love them so much and they were really keen for us to bring Big PUSH to South Africa. A few months later we welcomed Alfie Fabe who was also visiting from South Africa. Sometimes you meet people and it is as though you have known them all of your life and Alfie was one of those people. Early in the meeting Alfie gave us a prophetic word and an invitation to minister in Cape Town, South Africa and to bring Big PUSH. It looked like God wanted us to go to South Africa!

The first time we step into a nation has always been very significant and so we waited for God's timing to ensure that we would be with the right people, in the right place, at the right time. Fourteen months later Norma Dean, Pam Shaw, Tina and Colin Grant, and I were on our way to Cape Town, South Africa. When allocating the seats for our flights, I felt led to leave a spare seat next to Pam and I on the first leg of our journey as we flew towards Paris. I wondered what God was going to do?

A lovely young man came and dropped into the empty seat and quickly introduced himself as Andrew from Washington DC. We had a lovely chat about Andrew's life as he now lives in France and had just been visiting his family in Sheffield. We got around to his spiritual life and I shared my story with him. Just then the flight attendant came around to offer us snacks and a glass of wine. As a team we love to take communion together wherever we are and especially when we are travelling. So we took the bread and the wine to share communion together and we invited Andrew to join us, as you do when you are flying 39,000 feet above the earth, and he happily joined in.

My first book, Extravagant Fire, had just been published a couple of days earlier and we had packed a few books to distribute in South Africa. I took a copy out and wrote a personal message to Andrew - my first international book signing and my first book to go into France!

As we flew out of Paris, it was a beautiful clear night as we rose through the French skies. It was a thrill to see my first sighting of the Eiffel Tower as it was lit up in the midst of the darkness.

We arrived to a very warm welcome with Alfie, Mario, Harold, Marlena, Gary and Cheryl, cheering and waving the Union Jack with great gusto. Wow, what a great welcome and start to our time in South Africa!

We were staying and ministering within Mitchells Plain, located 32 km from Cape Town and an area originally constructed to house the coloured communities by the Apartheid government. This is now South Africa's third largest township and is home for up to 290,000 precious people. Sadly, now it has some of the largest ghettos and slum areas, where huge gangs operate, stalking the streets and controlling lives. Many people here are trapped in lifestyles of drug and alcohol addiction, paid for through selling their bodies, through pimps and violence. AIDs and HIV have spread rampantly, with many people dying prematurely. For many, life has become hopeless, while the struggle to simply survive the day is completely exhausting.

The area experiences an abnormally high murder rate due to the gang initiations that require people to shoot someone before they can be accepted into the gangs. Just before we arrived the gang warfare had been so violent that eight people had been killed in just one day.

However, the Churches are vibrant and full of life, courageously prepared to take a stand to see their communities transformed. We were pleased to be able to have an opportunity to serve our precious friends in their communities and their nation. We were escorted to our hosts; Pam and Norma stayed with Harold and Marlene, I stayed with Alfie and Lena, and Colin and Tina stayed with Stephen and Penny a few doors away. Tina, Colin and I were taken out for lunch and then not only did we have our first sighting of the ocean, we experienced our first paddle in the shark-infested waters - needless to say we did not go in too deep!

Wednesday was our first full day and Mario (a friend of Alfie's and now a friend of ours) drove us to meet Gary and Cheryl for our visit to Robben Island. The ferry journey was wonderful with the sun shining brightly and a great view of the Cape Town harbour and Table Mountain. The ferry takes 40 minutes to cross to the island and we were both thrilled and challenged to explore the place made famous by Nelson Mandela and his colleagues.

We were led around by a precious man who had been imprisoned there himself. He told us stories of the brutality and deprivation that went on there, which makes Nelson Mandela's story all the more amazing, as he came out and operated in such a spirit of grace and forgiveness. Nelson Mandela had every reason to be bitter and angry.

We heard from Cheryl that there was a Pastor from Cape Town who ministered on Robbin Island every week for seven years. He said that Nelson Mandela never missed one service in the seven years. The Pastor's very first message was about Joseph. He said this, "Maybe one of you sitting here is like a Joseph and maybe you will become the President of South Africa."

When Nelson Mandela became President, the Pastor told that story and that he had not known at the time that what he had said was so prophetic.

I picked up from the trip the sense of the price that was paid for freedom; freedom that we already have and most of us take for granted every day. What do we do with our freedom? Do we actually make the most of the opportunities we have whilst we enjoy that freedom?

We then enjoyed time with our friends Gary, Cheryl and Mario, having lunch in a lovely restaurant overlooking the harbour. Suffering for mission!

On Thursday morning we were introduced to Gerald who is a local Councillor in Cape Town. Gerald kindly offered to spend the day with us and to take us to the National Assembly Parliament Buildings and some other significant governmental places. We were half way to the Cecil Rhodes memorial, when a couple of the team realised that they had forgotten their passports, which they would need to get access into the Parliament building. So we had to double back to collect them. This meant that we were later arriving than we had wanted to be. I have learned to recognise that God knows what He is doing and these things often happen to ensure we are on time for His divine appointments.

We visited the Cecil Rhodes Memorial, which is located on Devil's Peak, part way up Table Mountain and overlooking the whole of Cape Town. The views from there are incredible and you can see right across the bay and the Atlantic Ocean. Cecil Rhodes was British and a leading Freemason; no surprise there. He had a strong influence over the formation of the government at the time and from the words on the statue, still did! We spent a powerful time there in prayer and certainly were aware of God's timing, as there was a general election just two weeks later. Interestingly, just as we were at the memorial statue on the side of Table Mountain, Cheryl and Gary were led by the Lord to pray at a similar but smaller statue of Cecil Rhodes, just outside of the Parliament Building.

As we prepared to go into the South African Parliament area, Gary and Cheryl joined us. We realised once again that God's timing is always perfect and we came to see why the passport delay was so significant. Gerald had told us that there was a major emergency inquiry going on in Parliament that morning to investigate President Zuma's excessive spending on his residence. Apparently, he has four wives and has spent millions of Rands of public funds building homes within his compound for each one of them, complete with tunnels to his private rooms so that nobody would know which wife was in with him at any particular time. Stephen Swartz MP needed to attend this meeting and there was a possibility that he may not be there to take us in. However, as we arrived we were thrilled to be greeted by Stephen and to discover that the meeting had just finished. I love God's timing!

Stephen is an incredible man of God and has been in Parliament for about 15 years. He has wonderful insight on spiritual matters and a powerful anointing for government. Stephen introduced us to Pastor Daniel Kleinbooi, who is the Pastor of Greenwood Park Baptist Church, Durban. Daniel was meeting with Stephen to explore how he could support the work of Parliament as a Chaplain. Stephen took us to some significant areas to pray and then we were privileged to go into the main parliamentary chamber. I wondered about the stories this chamber could tell us, all the political battles that had been won and lost. All the decisions that had been made here, that had brought incredible changes to this once broken nation.

This was our moment in history and we had it all to ourselves. So we made the most of the opportunity to pray and prophecy. We had a very powerful time together and this is some of the word we brought to them:

"I saw 2 young lions, about 6 months old, and they were watching you very carefully from a few yards away. At the moment they play together and it is difficult to tell their destinies apart, but one will go on to have a very significant role in leading the pride, while the other

will always be looking for opportunities to undermine and overthrow him. I felt The Lord is saying that he has given many young people a heart to govern, but they need to be taught and mentored to do it in the right way. They have to learn to have a heart after God and not just a heart for power. They need to be taught to follow the TRUTH, to have a passion for JUSTICE and INTEGRITY."

There was more but it would not be appropriate for me to share that here. However we did share the story of our visit to the British Treasury and prayed for the release of the multiplication anointing upon them. We received some wonderful encouragement from Stephen and Daniel who were thrilled with our visit and keen to stay in touch.

That evening we met with about twenty-five Intercessors and some leaders from across the Churches at Cape Town Vineyard Church. We hugged them all as we arrived and people commented on our love and unity right from the start. We shared our journey with them and some of the amazing things that have happened as God has answered our prayers. They were then given an opportunity to ask some questions and we did our best to answer them. We finished our time together by praying and releasing an impartation of what we carry to them all. They asked us to come back and we are planning to see them all again next time!

Friday was a gorgeous day and we had a day off to visit some beauty spots with Mario. One of the places we visited was Signal Point which is a high place overlooking the bay. It is a great place as you can see Robben Island in one direction and Table Mountain on the other. People were parachuting from the top and I thought about it for a moment. "Should I?" No I think I should give it a miss this time!"

On Saturday, we were ministering at a conference where they had an amazing gift of hospitality. The smells as we walked through the doors were lovely as we first encountered home-made "sisters", a kind of very tasty doughnut with coconut. I spoke about transforming our communities and we had an hilarious fire tunnel. We created the fire tunnel by bringing all of the prayer ministry team out to the front together and standing them in two lines facing each other. They stretched out their hands creating an arch and we invited the congregation to walk through from one end of the tunnel to the other, and as they did they received prayer. The prayer ministry team released the power and a fresh impartation of the fire of God over each person as they came through.

They had never experienced a fire tunnel before so we had great fun with the Holy Spirit, as many people were deeply touched, including one of the men who had great difficulty getting off the floor despite several attempts. As he came past me in the tunnel I could see a powerful anointing on him as a Pastor. However he had not been introduced as one of the Pastors so I did not saying anything. A few moments later as they were trying to close the meeting, they invited this man to close the meeting in prayer and they called him Pastor. This precious man rose to his feet, stretched out his hand and then immediately fell down backwards on to the floor in hysterical laughter without praying a word. Great joy broke out and many people were impacted. The Holy Spirit is so amazing and He loves releasing His joy!

On our first Sunday, the team split into three, with Tina and Colin ministering together. Norma and Pam went to minister in another Church. I ministered at "Tell Them Ministries" a Church led by Pastor Peter John. Gary and Cheryl came with me and helped with the times of prayer ministry and impartation. It was a thrill to be invited to Pastor Peter's home particularly as they had prepared a family feast in our honour.

Later that day we were welcomed to the first night of the conference, hosted by Llewellyn Williams who despite his name, was not Welsh. We enjoyed some very powerful worship before Norma taught on the Watchman, Intercessor and Gatekeeper, which was brilliant and very well received.

On Monday, we visited a Cheetah Sanctuary that I had seen on the television, a couple of months before we flew out to Cape Town. It was only about twenty minutes drive away from where we were staying, so it was too good an opportunity to miss. Despite us all being a little nervous, we enjoyed the experience of actually going into the enclosure with two nine-month old cheetah cubs. They were so cute and certainly made the loudest purring sounds I have ever heard! What a great experience to stroke these magnificent animals that have become so rare in the wild. I really expected them to be smooth and silky, however their coats were very coarse. But wow, we stroked real cheetahs!

Later in the evening we had the second night of the conference with Colin speaking on the joy of the Lord with a great time of impartation! Everyone was laughing and you could tell they had not experienced the Holy Spirit moving amongst them like that before. What a wonderful time of blessings.

Pam and Norma spent a day visiting the work led by Constance and Mercia. They are involved in working with a precious team of people who feed the poor and look after the really broken. For many people it may be the only hot meal they get for that week. Lots of their guests suffer desperately due to AIDs and HIV. This is rampant across these communities because of the inappropriate lifestyles where people have so many casual sexual partners. Pam and Norma prayed for so many people over several hours, including a young man who had a nasty leg wound from being shot in the last couple of days. We were thrilled to be able to release some funds into this amazing ministry.

On Wednesday we hired a car to travel to connect with a Church called OpenWell based in Mossel Bay. The journey was stunning as we drove up through the mountains shrouded in the early morning mist, on the Garden Route. We stayed with James and Marlize Oosthius and his lovely family overnight and had a precious time of fellowship with them.

The next day the Lord had some wonderful surprises in store for us as we drove out of Mossel Bay. Gary had suggested we stop off nearby at the Zorgfontein Game Lodge. Gary knew of my love for elephants and we arrived just as three beautiful elephants had come to the Lodge to be fed. Elephants yeah!

There was a large wooden raised platform attached to the side of the Lodge and the hungry elephants came and stood alongside. We stepped down on to the platform to feed them from a huge bucket of apples. I have to say it was impossible to keep up with their ravenous appetites. Their trunks were tough, with long spikes on and could take hold of the fruit and get it into their mouths at ninety miles an hour! I was so thrilled as I had never fed elephants before. God really loves to treat us.

Gary still had one surprise up his sleeve for us as we drove for a few more minutes to our next destination. We jumped out of our vehicles with a couple of minutes to spare before we were booked into walk with lions! Real lions! To be honest I was under the impression they would be little cuddly cubs, but it soon dawned on me that the approaching lions were not cubs and they were not little!

Tina, Colin, Pam and I had opted to go on this walk, but as our walking partners were approaching we wondered if we had made the right decision. We were given a long wooden stick each, a bit like a large walking stick, with clear instructions by the men looking after the lions. "If the lions attack you, do not run!" DO NOT RUN! You have got to be joking! "If they attack you," the man said, "just tap them on the nose with your stick".

I wondered, "What have we let ourselves in for?" My heart was pounding as we walked towards the Rangers and their rather large and very dangerous pussycats. The Rangers were really lovely and caring and soon put us at ease. Well, as much at ease as you can be with two huge lions a few inches away! They told us a little bit about the two lions, who had both been born in captivity and had lived with the Rangers from just one week old. The male was magnificent, big and strong. Yet he reminded me so much of Aslan from Narnia. He looked so kind and gentle. However, we later found out that he could roar very loudly and turn towards us very quickly! He and the female alongside him were just over three years old but knew what was expected of them. We walked a short distance before the lions jumped on to some logs and stood looking at us all. We managed to get some great photographs and then we were invited to come and stand a little closer.

I anxiously thought, "Are you kidding me!" However, each one of us in turn went to stand a little closer and had our photographs taken with them behind us. It was very scary, to look at the camera, when you knew there were two real live, fully grown, very strong lions with big teeth, standing just a couple of feet behind you, with no bars to separate you from being eaten. Oh my word!

After that we relaxed into the walk, as you do when you are walking with lions! They led the way and we followed them around a clear route, pausing along the way for further opportunities for photographs. Our beautiful companions posed once again, the female jumped onto a large log and stood regally whilst the male positioned himself lying down at the end of the log. They kept their eyes on the Rangers who had small pieces of meat on the end of the sticks to encourage them. One of the Rangers stepped forward and stood alongside the female, with the male now positioned at his feet. He began to stroke the female and we all watched in awe.

He asked, "Would you like to come and stroke her?" I thought, "What? You really want us to come and stroke a real live, fully grown lioness, with a male in a position where he could bite our legs off in an instant?"

"Ok then." After all you cannot miss an opportunity like that can you? So we took it in turn to go and stand next to the lioness and stroke her. Wow! We had lots of photographs taken which we need to keep looking at to remind us that we actually did walk with lions.

We walked about half way around when one of the Rangers jumped forward and jerked his stick quickly. He declared, "I have just flicked a baby cobra snake out of the way." Oh my goodness! I was so busy thinking about the lions that I had not even considered that there could be snakes. I quickly thanked God for keeping us safe and prayed that Mummy or Daddy Cobra would not be too upset that we had just flicked their little darling through the air.

Around the next corner there was an open space with a lovely tree in the middle. We watched the lioness clamber up on to one of the branches where she rested for a couple of minutes before leaping down right in front of us. Actually she could have jumped down right on top of us and killed us in a few moments. I am so glad she decided not to!

Thankfully, we survived the walk with a real sense of the amazing privilege we had experienced. God spoke to me very clearly and said, *"We need to remember that every day we can walk with the Lion of the Tribe of Judah.* (The Bible describes Jesus as the 'Lion of the tribe of Judah' in Revelation 5:5) *He has given us a rod of authority to carry and use when we are walking with Him. He has His angels walking ahead of us, to keep a watch over the enemy and to flick Him out of the way if he gets too close to us. The angels are there on duty to keep us safe when we are walking with Him."*

I will certainly never forget that and just to make sure I do not, I have had the photograph taken, of me stroking the lioness and the male roaring by my feet printed to remind me.

Saturday morning I was honoured to attend and speak at a Church Leaders prayer gathering in Mitchells Plain. The Leaders had been gathering together in response to the recent major increase in gang warfare. The Leaders worshipped and prayed with such passion and determination to see an end to the violence. I spoke to them about our experience with DrugsNET and how God had transformed Liverpool from the "drugs distribution capital of the UK" to the European Capital of Culture through mobilising the Church to pray! I was able to email them later with my notes with a copy of the DrugsNET strategy and prayer targets, which could be easily adapted to any community and situation. (Details of this are in Extravagant Fire).

Sadly we could not stay to the end of the meeting as we were whisked off to speak at another conference a few miles away. We heard later from Alfie that the Leaders had been deeply impacted by what I had shared and encouraged to continue to press into God until they saw the breakthrough come for them.

We enjoyed a morning of teaching people about the Prophetic which had been neglected in this community for far too long. We had great fun during the activations and prepared the way for a full prophetic training program in the near future.

That evening we helped our precious friends Llewellyn Williams, his family and friends to launch the South African Big PUSH. This was an amazing evening as we tried to model the Big PUSH style of gathering whilst enabling, empowering and encouraging them to discover what God has for them. The evening was well attended from across Mitchells Plain and Cape Town.

Part way through the evening the Lord spoke clearly to me about repentance and reconciliation regarding the season of Apartheid. He asked me to find three people who would be willing to represent the black, the white and the coloured communities. I spoke to our friend Mario, as he knew most people there and would be able to find the right people. A few minutes later Mario appeared with three amazing people who were willing to represent their different communities.

Just to be clear about what we were going to pray about: "Apartheid" actually means the state of being apart. This was the system of racial segregation prevalent across South Africa from 1948 to 1994 due to enforced legislation by the National Party governments.[1] The black, the white and the coloured communities would never have been able to meet together in the past. South Africa has come a long way since those days, however you do not have to dig too far, to see the pain and bitterness that is still there under the surface.

A couple of them shared a little of the horror stories of what they had experienced in the past and the fruit of what had happened to them. For example, Harold came out to the front to represent the coloured community. He spoke of having lots of land and property until some white people came and took it all, leaving them with nothing. You can understand why the coloured communities are still so angry without God's help to restore them. These three beautiful people apologised, standing in the gap on behalf of their people. It was a deep time of prayer as they poured out repentance to God and apologised to everyone there. There were a lot of tears from most people present, before people began to reach out to each other with sincere forgiveness. As people were praying for one another, the Lord whispered *"Ask them if they are willing to have their feet washed?"*

With Mario's help, I quietly asked if they would all be willing to have their feet washed. Thankfully they were, so we asked Latasha, Mario's lovely wife, if she could find some bowls of water and towels. Just before we started the process of washing their feet, another lady appeared and asked if she could come out to represent the Indian community, as they had also been very badly treated.

A few minutes later, I invited people to come and participate in the process of washing the feet of these precious people. By now most people were crying and some were sobbing uncontrollably. Over a dozen people came out from every community and fell to their knees in front of those who were about to have their feet washed. Many people gathered around with their cameras to record what was happening as clearly they had not participated in anything like this before. We knew this act of repentance and forgiveness was not just about four people having their feet washed. This was about whole communities receiving forgiveness and being able to move into their destinies as individuals, as communities and as a nation.

Some of the testimonies that have come from this session have been so encouraging. One came from the lady who had come out to represent the Indian community. She had suffered with a lot of pain in her foot for some time and the doctors had not been able to discover what the problem was. However after she had been involved in the process of repentance and reconciliation, including having her feet washed, she discovered a large spike from a plant had been buried deep in her foot. The spike broke through the skin and came right out before her eyes. Her walk was not just changed by a spike being removed from her foot, but by having her heart washed by the Holy Spirit.

One of the Ministers there had his feet washed by a white woman on her knees weeping before him. He was sobbing and later came to tell us what had happened to him. He had experienced a massive personal breakthrough as God had broken the lid off his anger and bitterness. As his feet were washed he knew the pain and the anger from the past had been washed away too. He felt completely different as the burden he had been carrying for so long was lifted off his shoulders.

Llewellyn said *"A big thank you to you and your team for the amazing anointing you guys were so willing to share with us and our ministries. We were blessed beyond words and more into action. Thanks Sue, it was such an awesome conference and you guys have a wonderful spirit."*

Helen said *"So sad to see you leaving as you have really opened heavens doors."*

Elsabe said, *"You and your team were a great blessing to us and I believe you have lifted the spirit of lethargy off this region."*

There were many more stories and no doubt more than we have been told. I really love it, when we do not know what to do but the Holy Spirit shows up and leads the way to breakthrough. We give God all the glory for what was done that day.

On Sunday morning our little team divided and we were blessed to minister in three lovely Churches before flying home later that evening. Norma and Pam had a very special experience as they went along to minister in the Children and Youth Church, which Harold, Marlene and their son have pioneered. This Church is an unusual Church as it is in the covered yard area of their home and is actually led by the children and young people. The youngsters all come from very poor homes with no other Christian input. Several of them are from Muslim homes and many have been neglected. Norma and Pam came away very inspired by what they had witnessed and by the children's vision to have a building of their own in the future.

South Africa felt like home for us and we felt as though there had been a massive shift in lives, in Churches and in the community. Thank you Lord!

1. Encyclopaedia Britannica

PARTNERSHIPS

We have learnt that as we are obedient in the little things God calls us to do, they align us for the greater things that God has in store for us. It has been essential to recognise how God speaks to us and to allow Him to guide us. We have learnt the importance of not holding back and waiting until we have had dozens of confirmations. We have learnt that we need to be obedient even when it does not make any natural sense to us. After all, receiving four pieces of coal led us to the nations and to some places of government that you could never ever imagine gaining access to. We would never have been able to do the things we have done without our extravagant God making them possible.

> *"I will proclaim the Lord's decree: He said to me, "You are my son; today I have become your father. Ask me and I will make the nations your inheritance, the ends of the earth your possession."* Psalm 2:7

I have shared about some of our adventures across the nations, but we have also had some amazing times here in the UK.

We love to work in partnership particularly inspired by these verses:

"One day as Jesus was standing by the Lake of Gennesaret, the people were crowding around him and listening to the word of God. He saw at the water's edge two boats, left there by the fishermen, who were washing their nets. He got into one of the boats, the one belonging to Simon, and asked him to put out a little from shore. Then he sat down and taught the people from the boat.

When he had finished speaking, he said to Simon, "Put out into deep water, and let down the nets for a catch." Simon answered, "Master, we have worked hard all night and have not caught anything. But because you say so, I will let down the nets." When they had done so, they caught such a large number of fish that their nets began to break. So they signalled to their partners in the other boat to come and help them, and they came and filled both boats so full that they began to sink." Luke 5

What great verses! There are some very simple principals here; no matter what the circumstances look like DO WHAT GOD TELLS YOU! As the disciples put their nets down in the deep waters they caught a huge catch of fish. However, they would not be able bring them to shore without the help of their partners. I love partnerships and we have developed several as we serve other groups and Church networks around the UK.

IPSWICH

I told the story of DrugsNET in my first book Extravagant Fire, but I did not tell you about what happened when I visited Ipswich. I was invited by a lovely friend Liz Beaton, who works with some of the Churches in the area. Liz had managed to assemble an amazing group of people from the local churches, the Police and the health authorities. I spoke for a little while and invited them all to see how they could partner with each other to impact their communities.

A little while later, Sergeant Neil Boast had a good idea, "To get the God squad out on the streets". Before long he was working with Liz and many others from the local Churches as they launched Town Pastors. The Town Pastors had just launched when Ipswich became the focus of all of the world's media, because of the horrendous and brutal murders of five girls who worked on the streets. The Town Pastors were there mobilising prayer and supporting the families, the Police and the other street girls.

Town Pastors were so successful in Ipswich that they spread right across Suffolk. They have won many awards and everywhere they have served their communities the crime rate has been reduced. I was very pleased to be visited by Neil Boast after he had retired. He had just been awarded an MBE for his amazing work across Suffolk and he really deserved it. Congratulations Neil, I am so proud of you!

MIDDLESBROUGH AND TEES VALLEY

We have been serving three Churches, St Georges, Christ Church and One Life Church. We love their leaders Julian and Helen Blakely, Robert and Sandra Hughes, Ian and Carol Graham. We have visited them several times over the last few years to help with teaching, empowering, activation in prayer and the prophetic.

One Sunday morning the Holy Spirit came very powerfully whilst we were gathered together as three Churches in Christ Church. This is the most traditional of the Churches and as we welcomed the Holy Spirit He came. Several of us actually felt the floor shaking and it was difficult to speak at all. Most of the service was abandoned as the Holy Spirit took over touching people in many different ways. Some people were crying out to God for revival to come, whilst others were weeping in repentance and others were receiving breakthroughs. That weekend several people were healed from bad knees, painful backs, stiff necks and problem feet. Awesome God!

We had a couple of people there that weekend who came along to check us out. They had invited us to speak at the Christian Police Association National Conference. We did not know what they looked like, so I had asked Norma to watch out for them. When I asked if anyone needed healing, several people came forward for prayer. God was moving upon people very powerfully and as I stretched out my hand to pray for one man who had an Achilles Heel problem, he crashed to the floor. God was at work in him and when he picked himself up from the floor, he declared he was healed. It turned out that this was Sergeant Brian McCarthy, one of the men who had come to check us out!

We had no idea what to expect, a few weeks later, when we arrived to speak at the Christian Police Association National Conference. The conference was attended by Police Officers from every rank and from across the nation, representing almost every force area.

We were really pleased that the Holy Spirit had decided to come along too. As I got up to speak I welcomed His presence and He came so powerfully. Once again it was difficult to move or to speak, with many people in floods of tears as He was touching people with His deep love. There was a huge response from people after we had shared from the scriptures about their spiritual authority. Thankfully, what we did not know was that we were being marked! I am glad I did not know that before. This is what Brian said later:

"I have the great privilege of saying thank you for your support at the conference in Cleveland. It is always a pleasure to spend time with you ladies, you are an inspiration and a great example of lives spent walking with God.

I do not know if you are aware, I asked for feedback from the delegates who attended the conference. Would it surprise you to hear that 95% of the delegates who responded awarded you ten out of ten for your presentation and prayer workshop? That means out of a maximum possible 430 points you were awarded 410! This is phenomenal by anyone's standards. In addition, respondents said that your presentation was the highlight of the conference for them. On both counts this is more than any other aspect of the conference, even though other guest speakers also scored phenomenally!

I have to say that the recorded feedback entirely reflects the verbal response from delegates. There were so many excited people who had heard you, received prayer or words of knowledge that I lost count. People are hungry for God. Thank you, thank you, thank you!"

We have also ministered at the Tees Valley Forum, where it was wonderful to meet so many inspiring Christians all involved in serving their local communities.

We continue to see Ian and Carol Graham regularly as they come across to Liverpool most months to attend the Big PUSH. Ian and Carol, we love you x

HAWICK AND JEDBURGH

We first met Charles Finnie and his lovely wife Lynne a few years ago. We were thrilled to be invited to minister in their Church, in the Burnfoot area of Hawick.

Earlier in the year, Norma had a prophetic word from Jeremiah 12:5, *"If you have raced with men on foot and they have worn you out, how can you compete with the horses?"*

Prior to us visiting Hawick, we were at a meeting in Edinburgh and I asked Norma to look out for Graham and Eunice Astle, as we would be ministering in their Church in Jedburgh on Sunday evening. During the meeting there was a call for Leaders to receive prayer and there was a big response. I would normally have gone to minister to them straight away, but the Lord told me to take a step back and so I waited. The Lord pointed a man out to me and said, "He is the one I want you to pray for". I stepped towards this man and looked at his name badge. This was Graham Astle. I love the Holy Spirit's introductions!

At the end of the meeting Charles said he had a surprise in store for us that evening. We travelled to Hawick where we went out for a meal with Charles, Lynne, Marion and Joyce, before we were taken into Hawick town centre. We had arrived in the middle of the Common Riding season and the riders were just about to arrive back in town. It was not too long before we could hear the pounding of hooves, lots and lots and lots of hooves all heading in our direction. Suddenly at the top of the hill, the first of the riders appeared followed by big horses and little horses, hundreds of horses and riders of every size and description.

This was a real sign to us that we were in the right place, at the right time, with the right people. It turns out that 499 years ago there had been a huge battle, the Battle of Flodden when most of the adult males had been killed. Some months later, a group of young Scottish men stole into the English camp and took their flag while the English army was sleeping. The flag has remained in Scotland ever since. On the anniversary of the flag being stolen in 1514 the people of the Borders continue to ride out to ensure that the English are not attempting to return. We joked that we were there to retrieve the flag and to take it back to England, but we did not say it too loudly!

We had a great weekend and God's presence was so strong. We ministered in Hawick on Sunday morning and in Jedburgh in the evening and we had a lot of fun with the Holy Spirit! You will have to read between the lines here, as I am not going to tell you all that happened.

Transforming change began to happen here as people began to pray. The local school was affected as one of the teachers went into the building, praying and releasing the goodness of God into the classrooms. The behaviour of the children notably changed and they no longer got into trouble or had fights in the playground. The school was no longer vandalised, saving on maintenance budgets and heartache. The Lord cared about those children so much that he provided sufficient funds for the Church to take most of the class away for a weekend. Many of those children had never been away from home before and now they also go along to the children's club at Church. Can you imagine the impact on the future of those children and their families?

We have continued to visit Hawick and Jedburgh to minister each year. 2014 was the 500th Anniversary and we were there to help them celebrate in style. We were very pleased to hear that the English flag was actually restored back to England a few weeks later.

THANET

Returning to Kent was a real pleasure for me as I had spent the early years of my married life there. Julie Wickenden and Honor Todd, who have been involved in prayer in Thanet for some years, invited us there In 2014 we returned for our second visit and experienced some interesting phenomena.

We arrived on Friday and we visited their Prayer House located a few streets away. As we were praying for them there I began to prophecy over them, *"The glass ceiling is coming down! It is coming down! Right now the glass ceiling is coming down!"* I knew that the Lord was speaking about the invisible ceiling that is over many lives and especially women, preventing them from fully reaching their potential. It is usually never spoken about and is often so subtle, but it hinders and stunts life in so many ways.

As we stepped out of the Prayer House, Julie's phone rang and it was her husband Malc. To everyone's shock and surprise, the dining room ceiling in Malc and Julie's home had just collapsed at exactly the time I was prophesying the ceiling was coming down! Norma, Steve and I were staying in Malc and Julie's, and by the time we got back to their home there was a huge hole in the ceiling five feet wide. If that was not enough, the next day there was a tornado in their community and Christ Church in Ramsgate was struck by lightening. Oh my goodness!

We enjoyed spending time teaching and ministering to the precious people of Thanet. It was wonderful to see people awakening to who they really are and what can happen when they partner with God.

The next week, 19th July 2014 we were back in Liverpool, for the Big PUSH. The theme of the Big PUSH was "Releasing the Wave" and I asked the Lord *"What is the wave you are wanting to release?"* The Lord said, *"It is a wave of My blessing."* That sounded good to us, so we stood together in Liverpool and released the waves of God's blessings across to the places that God had put into our hearts including Kent. A couple of days later I had an email from Simon, a friend from Kent, with details of a strange weather phenomenon that had happened on Saturday afternoon. He said, "I know this has something to do with you!" As I clicked on the link it was the coverage of a Tsunami Wave Cloud that had touched Kent.[1]

Then on 4th August 2014 there was another email with details of a further phenomenon, as another strange cloud formation in the form of a funnel appeared over Kent. This was reported on ITV News and the reporter asked, "Is this the Hand of God?"[2]

There has been so much talk of God judging the UK and I know that we deserve to be judged. However, I believe that God is looking for those who will stand in the gap so that He can release the blessings. The signs in the sky, including "the hand of God" reaching down to touch the earth, are signs to us to be ready and to align ourselves with Him.

PARTINGTON

In the past you could drive through Partington and not notice it at all. It is located between Lymm in Cheshire and Manchester, so it was easy for it to be overlooked. At first impression it was uncared for and broken.

We love Partington and have been pleased to support the work of the People's Church and St Mary's Church. We first went across there to provide a mini Prayer School hosted by the People's Church and once again the Lord moved very powerfully. Pastor Jonathan and his wife had just had a little boy and for the first three weeks of his life he was struggling to feed. This precious Mummy and Daddy were in and out of the hospital trying to resolve their new little's son's feeding problems. We laid hands on him and prayed, and instantly this beautiful little one was healed. There was great joy at his speedy recovery as he fed and thrived from that moment on.

Later we were invited to minister in St Mary's Church where Rev. Peter Geddes and his wife Liz lead the work. We had an extraordinary time, as once again the Holy Spirit moved in our midst very powerfully. He came with such power, that it was very difficult to speak and the tears flowed from many of the men and women. Five people gave their lives to Jesus that day, including a family of three who had come as part of their daughter's school project. She had to visit different faith groups to write a report and this particular week happened to be the turn of a Christian Church. They had come to St Mary's and encountered God's love.

We love the Geddes family and count them as precious friends. They also come across to the Big PUSH in Liverpool regularly and Simon their son has become a wonderful member of the CWM Team.

As God's people began to pray more effectively, the good news is that Partington began to change dramatically:

1. A team of people from The Message Trust's Eden Team moved in to live and love the community.

2. A friend of ours, Debra Green was offered The Fuse Building at a ridiculous price after those who had built it could not afford to run it. Debra is leading Redeeming Our Communities (ROC) from there now. How apt!

3. The very shabby Partington shopping area has been demolished and a new shopping centre is being constructed.

Lives are being changed by God's transforming love and we give Him all of the glory!

---

1 https://www.youtube.com/watch?v=8RI6HQUxVpU

2 https://www.youtube.com/watch?v=mHg3xzxFaKI

VICTORY'S SIDE

Liverpool continues to be in my heart. I think that if you cut me in half, I would have "I love Liverpool" right through the middle like a piece of Blackpool Rock. I love that we get to travel around our nation and the nations, but I always love coming back home to Liverpool.

In Liverpool we have dreamed of what our city would look like when it is transformed and now we are watching as it is changing before our eyes. We have been truly amazed by what has been happening in Liverpool and the surrounding region. God is doing something dynamic and we are seeing huge shifts in many areas. There are many new homes being built and two new hospitals; one to accommodate the new Alder Hey Children's Hospital and the other to replace the Royal Liverpool Hospital.

There is a new deep-water dock under construction to take even larger vessels. There are new hotels being built and opened up to keep up with the vast number of tourists arriving from all around the world. In 2015 we will welcome lots of cruise liners but we are particularly excited about the three Queens arriving. This will be the first time that the three luxury liners will be together anywhere in the world - the Queen Elizabeth, the Queen Mary 2 and the Queen Victoria, will bring 6000 tourists into the city to celebrate the 175th Anniversary of the Cunard Shipping Line. Liverpool will welcome thousands of tourists who will come to see this amazing sight. If we had told anybody even ten years ago that we would be welcoming luxury cruise liners into Liverpool, people would not have believed it would be possible.

We have become one of the most top performing retail centres with the new Liverpool One Shopping Centre leading the way. The Observer national newspaper called Liverpool "the most happening city."

Liverpool is on the map for many different reasons and it is not just the tourists who are coming. During the summer of 2014 the business leaders of the world assembled in Liverpool for the Global Economic Forum, and later the same year the International Festival for Business welcomed world leaders and they came to see the transformation of Liverpool. I was overwhelmed to hear that the Mayor of Cali, Columbia was one of those guests. Watching what God was doing in Cali, in the Transformation Video was where our journey began and now we were being visited by the Mayor of Cali to see the transformation in Liverpool!

We have seen God moving in power on the streets and parks too as we have talked and prayed with people. During one summer day in 2014, as I was in Bold Street with a team from "Jesus Loves Liverpool", I was so blessed to lead three people to Jesus, one after the other. Many people gave their lives to Jesus that day and many were healed. The next day we were in Newsham Park where there were lots of people enjoying the lovely sunshine. One person from the team had a word of knowledge about a sports injury to the knee that God wanted to heal. As this word was shared with a group of about twenty young people, one young man responded. He received prayer and instantly God healed him. Suddenly everyone wanted prayer and these young people were straight on their mobile phones to tell their friends what God had done. Many people were healed and many gave their lives to Jesus too. I love what God is doing and we give Him all of the glory!

There is still much work to be done and many issues remain to be dealt with. However we are not overwhelmed, as the Lord to guides and leads us.

"The Lord confides in those who fear Him; He makes His covenant known to them." Psalm 24:14

We want to be a people who have a reverential fear of the Lord; a people who are so close to God that we hear His heartbeat and He feels He can confide in us.

We thank God for what He is doing here in Liverpool and we look to Him for the completion of what has been started. We know that the Lord is going to release a new sound from here, the sound of the love of God, and this is going to be greater than anything the Beatles won acclaim for. We want Liverpool to be known as a place where the glory of God dwells.

I have shared our story in Liverpool to encourage you that God can take the most broken places and change them dramatically. Always remember that when things seem the worst, that is the greatest opportunity for God to turn things around and then all the glory goes to Him. He wants to use you to bless your community, city and nation. I encourage you to press into Him for the strategy and breakthrough for the people of your land.

Just to remind you we began our adventures with being led by the Holy Spirit. He showed us what to do and the issues that needed to be dealt with:

1. We started by understanding who we were.
2. We needed to understand our city's history and identify the main issues that needed to be dealt with and what had already been dealt with.
3. We needed to play our part to deal with the sin of the Slave Trade and the European carving up of Africa.
4. We apologised for the Heysel Disaster.
5. We visited the Hillsborough Stadium and never gave up praying to see Truth and Justice come after the Hillsborough Disaster.
6. Then the Lord opened the gates and gave us the authority we needed for us to go on our adventures. The Lord has used us powerfully and we

have been given some wonderful opportunities to share our experiences and release others to bring transformation in their communities.

"For the KINGDOM of God is not a matter of talk but of power."
1 Corinthians 4: 20

It is time for us as God's people to understand who we are, to walk with God and move in the power of the Holy Spirit. It is important for us to know what God has called us to do. It is time for us to seize the day and to take hold of the gifts that God has for us. It is time for us to ensure that the next generation walks in freedom and the fullness of all God has. It is time for us to move in the prophetic, the signs, wonders and miracles. It is time for us to be the spiritual Mothers and Fathers our communities and nations need. It is certainly time to LOVE, mentor, empower, encourage and release those around us to be all God created them to be.

Not only that, but we have seen many signs, wonders and miracles along the way too. From babies being born to people declared barren, to cancer disappearing, a £50 note appearing, debts being paid off, financial provision and a lost sapphire stone being recovered. There is always more for us and as we focus on making God's presence our priority, we begin to see that released.

"Now to him who is able to do IMMEASURABLY MORE than all we ask or imagine according to His POWER that is at work WITHIN US."
Ephesians 3:20

When we choose to believe God can do IMMEASURABLY MORE in our cities and nations by investing our faith in prophetic prayer, anything can and will happen.

"Live your truth.
Express your love.
Share your enthusiasm.
Take action towards your dreams.
Walk your talk.
Dance and sing to your music.
Embrace your blessings.
Make today worth remembering."
Dr. Steve Maraboli

In short Carpe Diem - "Seize the Day" - Let the adventures begin!

17 March 2011

Dear Mrs Sinclair,

I wanted personally to thank you and the members of your prayer meeting for the contribution you have made to reducing our excessive national debt. It is very much appreciated.

Best wishes.

George Osborne

SUE SINCLAIR

Sue Sinclair is married to Steve and has two children. Sue has served on the Sefton Local Strategic Partnership for eight years, as Prayer Co-ordinator for Christian networks Together For the Harvest and Merseyfest for several years as well as playing an active role in local church leadership.

Sue is a visionary and has pioneered many new ministries within the church and reaching out into the community. Sue has led CommUNITY Watchmen Ministries (CWM) since 2002; based in Merseyside CWM consists of Christians from across the North West and across the breadth of the Church.

CWM reaches out into the local communities, the region, the nation and across the nations. They minister throughout the UK, Europe and Africa. God has led them on many adventures taking them into places of government and giving them opportunities to pray for and give prophetic encouragement to international government Ministers.

Sue and the CWM team love to teach, empower and activate the Church and have a strong anointing to bring breakthrough. Sue is just an ordinary woman who is learning to walk with an amazing and awesome God.

SUE SINCLAIR

EXTRAVAGANT
FIRE

The fire of God's LOVE can change you!

This is Sue's first book and has had wonderful reviews.

EXTRAVAGANT FIRE uses the illustration of controlled burning that burns up all the dead wood, rot and decay causing dormant seeds to germinate. This controlled fire brings life and that is why it is extravagant fire.

Sue shares her journey through the EXTRAVAGANT FIRE to encountering the God of the miraculous. This includes how an amazing awesome God takes an ordinary dysfunctional woman and loves, cleanses and heals her before taking her into places of governmental power to bring shifts and changes. EXTRAVAGANT FIRE will bring you hope and raise your levels of expectation that God can and does use very ordinary people for extraordinary exploits.